Editor
Mara Ellen Guckian

Editor in Chief
Karen J. Goldfluss, M.S. Ed.

Cover Artist
Brandon DiAntonis

Illustrator
Renée Christine Yates

Art Coordinator
Renée Christine Yates

Imaging
Leonard P. Swierski

Publisher
Mary D. Smith, M.S. Ed.

Extraordinary Women

Clara Barton

Harriet Beecher Stowe

Christa McAuliffe

Eleanor Roosevelt

SUSAN B. ANTHONY 50¢ U.S. POSTAGE

Sojourner Truth

Teacher Created Resources

TCR 3209

Grades 5–8

Author
Robert W. Smith

Teacher Created Resources, Inc.
6421 Industry Way
Westminster, CA 92683
www.teachercreated.com

ISBN: 978-1-4206-3209-5

© 2009 Teacher Created Resources, Inc.
Made in U.S.A.

Teacher Created Resources

Table of Contents

Introduction

The *Spotlight on America* series is designed to introduce some of the seminal events in American history to students in the fifth through eighth grades. Reading in the content area is enriched with a balanced variety of activities in written language, literature, social studies, oral expression, science, art, and math. The series is designed to make history come alive in your classroom and take root in the minds of your students.

The great moral issue of the 19th century was slavery. The movement to abolish the institution of slavery became the first of several movements to secure equal rights for women, women's suffrage, and temperance (the elimination of alcoholism). Among the leading figures in each of these movements of the 19th and early 20th centuries were women reformers and advocates who shared the same core beliefs, although they sometimes differed in style, objectives, and methods. From the Civil War through 1920, the major emphasis was on women's suffrage, followed by efforts to help African Americans, factory workers, and child laborers. The major emphasis of the late 20th century focused on the civil rights and voting rights of African Americans and disadvantaged citizens.

The reading selections and comprehension questions in this book serve to introduce some of the women who were vital to the success of the United States as a nation. You will notice a number of different terms used when referring to different groups of people. In the present day, the indigenous peoples of the Americas are referred to as Native Americans. This term is generally used in this book, except where the historical context requires the use of Indian or American Indian. Similarly, African Americans is used except where it would be inappropriate due to the context. Negroes, blacks, freed slaves, and freedmen were respectable terms in the 19th and early 20th centuries. These groups were a driving force of an evolving democracy and especially important in the development of literature, poetry, and the arts.

Women became deeply involved in the extraordinary development of modern medicine, especially in the treatment of soldiers, women, children, and the disadvantaged. Women were among the earliest pioneers in aviation. Later, when the opportunity came, women joined men as astronauts traveling the new frontiers of space.

The readings in this book set the stage for activities in other subject areas. The literature readings are intended to immerse students into the lives of these extraordinary women. The activities in written language, poetry, biography, and research are designed to help students recognize and empathize with the lives of these pioneer American women. The dramatic opportunities in Readers' Theater and Famous Women impersonations will help all students figuratively walk in the footsteps of these women and the men who knew them. The activities with time lines, maps, and science provide students with a sense of time, place, and historical perspective. The culminating activities aim to give students a sense of living history.

Enjoy using this book with your students and look for other books in this series.

Teacher Lesson Plans for Reading Comprehension

Abolitionists

Objective: Students will demonstrate fluency and comprehension in reading historically-based text.

Materials: copies of Abolitionists (pages 7–9); copies of Abolitionists Quiz (page 34); additional reading selections from books, encyclopedias, and Internet sources for enrichment

Procedure:

1. Reproduce and distribute Abolitionists. Review pre-reading skills by briefly reviewing text and encouraging students to underline as they read, make notes in the margins, list questions, and highlight unfamiliar words as they read.

2. Have students read the article independently, in small groups, or together as a class.

3. As a class, discuss the following questions or others of your choosing.
   - How important do you think the publication of *Uncle Tom's Cabin* was to the abolitionist movement?
   - Which abolitionist leader do you most admire? Why?
   - Why do you think these women became involved in the abolitionist movement?
   - Do you think you would have been an abolitionist if you lived in the 1840s and 1850s? Explain your answer.

Assessment: Have students complete Abolitionists Quiz. Correct the quiz together.

Women's Suffrage and Native Americans

Objective: Students will demonstrate fluency and comprehension in reading historically-based text.

Materials: copies of Women's Suffrage (pages 10–13) and Women's Suffrage Quiz (page 35); copies of Native Americans (pages 14–15) and Native Americans Quiz (page 36); additional reading selections from books, encyclopedias, and Internet sources for enrichment

Procedure:

1. Reproduce and distribute Women's Suffrage and Native Americans. Review pre-reading skills by briefly reviewing text and encouraging students to underline as they read, make notes in the margins, list questions, and highlight unfamiliar words as they read.

2. Have students read the articles independently, in small groups, or together as a class.

3. As a class, discuss the following questions or others of your choosing.
   - Which suffragette do you most admire? Why?
   - Who was the most important suffragette? Why?
   - Which Native American woman would you most like to have known? What questions would you ask her?
   - Do you think you would have been a suffragette if you lived from the 1840s to 1920? Explain your answer.

Assessment: Have students complete Women's Suffrage Quiz and Native Americans Quiz. Correct the quizzes together.

Teacher Lesson Plans
for Reading Comprehension *(cont.)*

Reformers and Change Makers

Objective: Students will demonstrate fluency and comprehension in reading historically-based text.

Materials: copies of Reformers and Change Makers (pages 16–19); copies of Reformers and Change Makers Quiz (page 37); additional reading selections from books, encyclopedias, and Internet sources for enrichment

Procedure:

1. Reproduce and distribute Reformers and Change Makers. Review pre-reading skills by briefly reviewing text and encouraging students to underline as they read, make notes in the margins, list questions, and highlight unfamiliar words as they read.

2. Have students read the article independently, in small groups, or together as a class.

3. As a class, discuss the following questions or others of your choosing.
   - Which reformer do you most admire? What did she do that you admire?
   - Which of the women took the greatest risks? Explain your answer.
   - Which of the reformers accomplished the most?

Assessment: Have students complete Reformers and Change Makers Quiz. Correct the quiz together.

Scientists and Astronauts–Pioneers in Medicine

Objective: Students will demonstrate fluency and comprehension in reading historically-based text.

Materials: copies of Scientists and Astronauts (pages 20–22) and Scientists and Astronauts Quiz (page 38); copies of Pioneers in Medicine (pages 23–26) and Pioneers in Medicine Quiz (page 39); additional reading selections from books, encyclopedias, and Internet sources for enrichment

Procedure:

1. Reproduce and distribute Scientists and Astronauts and Pioneers in Medicine. Review pre-reading skills by briefly reviewing text and encouraging students to underline as they read, make notes in the margins, list questions, and highlight unfamiliar words as they read.

2. Have students read the articles independently, in small groups, or together as a class.

3. As a class, discuss the following questions or others of your choosing.
   - Which scientist, astronaut, or medical pioneer would you like to have known or worked with? Why?
   - Which of these women accomplished the most or helped people the most?
   - How does the work of people like Rachel Carson, Alice Hamilton, or Emma Willard affect your life today?

Assessment: Have students complete Scientists and Astronauts Quiz and Pioneers in Medicine Quiz. Correct the quizzes together.

Teacher Lesson Plans for Reading Comprehension *(cont.)*

Artists and Writers

Objective: Students will demonstrate fluency and comprehension in reading historically-based text.

Materials: copies of Artists and Writers (pages 27–30) and copies of Artists and Writers Quiz (page 40); additional reading selections from books, encyclopedias, and Internet sources for enrichment

Procedure:

1. Reproduce and distribute Artists and Writers. Review pre-reading skills by briefly reviewing text and encouraging students to underline as they read, make notes in the margins, list questions, and highlight unfamiliar words as they read.

2. Have students read the article independently, in small groups, or together as a class.

3. As a class, discuss the following questions or others of your choosing.
   * Which artist painted in a style that you like or had a life you found interesting?
   * Which writer or poet wrote about subjects which appealed to your interests? Whose books or poems would you like to read? Why?
   * Why are the achievements of Marian Anderson and Maria Tallchief important to women of any race or color?

Assessment: Have students complete Artists and Writers Quiz. Correct the quiz together.

First Ladies

Objective: Students will demonstrate fluency and comprehension in reading historically-based text.

Materials: copies of First Ladies (pages 31–33) and copies of First Ladies Quiz (page 41); additional reading selections from books, encyclopedias, and Internet sources for enrichment

Procedure:

1. Reproduce and distribute First Ladies. Review pre-reading skills by briefly reviewing text and encouraging students to underline as they read, make notes in the margins, list questions, and highlight unfamiliar words as they read.

2. Have students read the article independently, in small groups, or together as a class.

3. As a class, discuss the following questions or others of your choosing.
   * Which First Lady seemed to be most important to the success of her husband's presidency?
   * Which First Lady would have been a good president? Explain your choice.
   * What issues are important for First Ladies to discuss and support?
   * What leadership qualities should the first woman President of the United States possess? What issues should she support?

Assessment: Have students complete First Ladies Quiz. Correct the quiz together.

Reading Passages

Abolitionists

The great moral issue of the 19th century was slavery. The movement to abolish the institution of slavery was often led by determined women who were committed to this issue as well as other reforms.

Harriet Beecher Stowe (1811–1896)

"So you're the little lady who started this great big war," Abraham Lincoln told Harriet Beecher Stowe when they met in the White House. It wasn't that large an exaggeration.

In 1832 Harriet Beecher moved with her family to Cincinnati, Ohio. She soon became involved in the movement to abolish slavery when she saw first hand the effects of slavery and heard the stories of fugitive slaves who escaped from Kentucky and other Southern states.

Harriet became a schoolteacher and a successful, part-time writer of magazine articles and books. She married a widowed professor at Lane Theological Seminary, Calvin Stowe, and helped support her rapidly-growing family with her published stories. After they moved to Maine so her husband could teach at Bowdoin College, Harriet wrote a long novel about slavery called *Uncle Tom's Cabin*. It first ran as a series of stories in a monthly magazine. The stories were based on true accounts of slavery and escape that Harriet heard from fugitive slaves while living in Ohio.

The publication of *Uncle Tom's Cabin* in 1852 was a literary sensation. It sold a record 300,000 copies in the first year. The violence and mistreatment of slaves portrayed in the book caused many Northern people to reject slavery as an American institution. *Uncle Tom's Cabin* was a massively influential novel that hardened the positions of the antislavery North and the pro-slavery South. Harriet Beecher Stowe published many other books including another antislavery novel. She remained a respected speaker and literary figure until her death.

Reading Passages

Abolitionists *(cont.)*

Sarah Grimke (1792–1873)
Angelina Grimke (1805–1879)

The Grimke sisters were born and raised in a wealthy, slave-owning family in Charleston, South Carolina. Both girls in the large family became deeply opposed to the evils of slavery as young children. They soon rebelled against the culture of physical violence and mistreatment of blacks. First Sarah and later Angelina moved to Philadelphia and became members of the Quaker religion, which supported the abolition of slavery.

Both sisters became involved in writing letters opposed to the institution of slavery. Angelina addressed Southern women, and Sarah wrote a letter to Southern clergymen asking them to oppose slavery. The letters infuriated people in their hometown of Charleston, South Carolina, and even upset some Quakers who thought the young women were being too bold. The sisters began speaking in homes and churches urging women and sympathetic Northern men to become active in the movement to eradicate slavery.

Angelina married a famous abolitionist, Theodore Weld, and both sisters also became active supporters of women's suffrage. The sisters lived to see slavery ended with Union victory in the Civil War.

Sojourner Truth (c. 1797–1883)

"Children, I talk to God, and God talks to me." Sojourner Truth often began her remarkable speeches with these words. She was an electrifying orator who thrilled audiences with her message and presence as she lectured throughout the North and Midwest during the years preceding the Civil War.

Sojourner started life as a slave named Isabella in New York State. In her early life, she was sold several times before the New York Emancipation Act of 1827 freed her.

Although she could neither read nor write, Sojourner had always heard voices in her head. In 1843 she began a career as a wandering preacher and adopted the name Sojourner Truth. She soon became an advocate for the abolition of slavery and later spoke for women's suffrage and women's property rights. Her "Ain't I a Woman" speeches stressed the need to liberate both slaves and women from the legal and social bonds of the time. She helped gather funds for black soldiers, met Abraham Lincoln during the war, and tried to organize Western settlements for freed blacks after the Civil War.

Reading Passages

Abolitionists *(cont.)*

Harriet Tubman (c. 1820–1913)

Born one of 11 children in a slave family, Harriet Tubman was mistreated and beaten by her master who often rented her out to other people. She was once hit on the head so hard by an overseer she sustained a permanent injury. After that incident, she suffered a kind of drowsiness that affected her when she was not active. Finding that she and two of her brothers were going to be sold to another owner, Harriet decided to run away, even though her husband and brothers were reluctant to join her.

Harriet escaped from her owner in Maryland and got to Pennsylvania, a free state. Determined to help other slaves escape, Harriet established a route of Underground Railroad stations and made more than 20 trips into Southern states, rescuing her parents, two brothers, many members of her family, and more than 300 other slaves. Rewards for her capture posted by slave owners totaled over $40,000.

Harriet's determination to rescue her family and other slaves, her gritty courage, and her unwavering belief that all slaves should be free made her a symbol of liberty to oppressed slaves and to all people opposed to slavery. To Southern slave owners, Harriet was an emblem of the danger threatening their control of their human property.

Harriet became a famous antislavery speaker and activist and even helped John Brown recruit some of his followers. During the Civil War, Harriet served as a spy, scout, and nurse for the Union army. She set up her own home as a refuge for needy freed slaves after the war.

Other Abolitionists

Other women who campaigned effectively for the abolition of slavery were suffragettes Lucretia Mott, Susan B. Anthony, Elizabeth Cady Stanton, and Lucy Stone. Frances Wright tried to set up a colony of free slaves called Nashoba as a way of creating gradual emancipation. Maria Chapman published articles and provoked so much anger from a mob that they burned down a hall where she spoke.

Reading Passages

Women's Suffrage

The battle for women's suffrage consumed the energies of reformers for 80 years from 1840 to 1920 when the passage of the 19th Amendment to the Constitution ended that struggle. Within the context of the movement was the broader fight for equal property rights, advanced education, child custody, and equal treatment in divorce cases, along with reducing many of the social limitations placed upon the dress and behavior of women.

Elizabeth Cady Stanton (1815–1902)

"Ah! If you'd only been a boy!" Judge Cady often remarked to his daughter, Elizabeth. His sons had all died, and his daughter had many attributes that were wonderful in a boy but unwanted in a girl in those days. Elizabeth was extremely independent, and she insisted on studying Greek and the law. She was the top student and the only girl in her academy. Elizabeth was unable to attend college because no college accepted girls, but she did attend Emma Willard's Female Seminary.

Her father didn't like Henry Stanton who asked Elizabeth to marry him. Henry was 10 years older than Elizabeth, not financially secure, and was an abolitionist. They eloped and were married, but, in the marriage ceremony, Elizabeth refused to promise she would obey him. Along with her husband, she became involved in many liberal movements of the day, especially the abolition of slavery. She became concerned with the second-rate status of women even in these movements.

In 1831 Elizabeth met Susan B. Anthony and they would remain colleagues in the long struggle to obtain property rights for women, easier divorce laws for women married to violent or drunken men, and especially the right to vote. Elizabeth often wrote Susan's speeches while Susan helped care for

Elizabeth's seven children. They founded a newspaper called *Revolution*, wrote books, and formed associations to carry on the long battle for suffrage. In 1848, Elizabeth and Lucretia Mott issued a call for a women's rights convention in Seneca Falls, New York. Her *Declaration of Sentiments*, a declaration of rights for women, became the standard for the women's rights movement during the long 80-year drive for women's suffrage.

Elizabeth was also a strong supporter of the Emancipation Proclamation, suffrage for freed blacks of both genders, and the temperance movement against alcohol addiction.

Elizabeth Cady Stanton and Susan B Anthony

Reading Passages

Women's Suffrage *(cont.)*

Susan B. Anthony (1820–1906)

Susan B. Anthony had a Quaker upbringing in Massachusetts and New York. She taught in a Quaker seminary and was headmistress of an academy for girls. She met many of the leading abolition leaders of her day when she returned to her family home in central New York State. She also supported the temperance movement. Susan met Amelia Bloomer and Elizabeth Cady Stanton, and became a zealous and outspoken advocate for suffrage, women's property rights, the emancipation of slaves, and inclusion of women in the 14th Amendment granting Negro suffrage.

Susan B. Anthony was the focus of ridicule, abuse, and severe criticism from politicians, newspapers, and the general public because her speeches, lectures, and writings were unsettling to the conservative forces in society. She was even the target of stones thrown by gangs of boys when she wore "bloomers" to promote more sensible women's clothing.

Susan was active in supporting suffrage movements in California, Michigan, Colorado, and other states. Susan voted illegally in the 1872 presidential election in Rochester, New York, and was arrested, jailed, convicted, and fined. She refused to pay the fine but was released from jail anyway.

By 1890 Susan B. Anthony had overcome the general public's anger and personal animosity, and became a respected national heroine. She worked with Carrie Chapman Catt to carry on the task of passing a constitutional amendment for women's suffrage. With her longtime friend and colleague, Elizabeth Cady Stanton, Susan wrote a four-volume history of the women's movement. The 19th Amendment conferring the right of women to vote was passed in 1920. In 1979 she was the first woman depicted on U.S. currency, a dollar minted in her honor.

Amelia Bloomer (1818–1894)

Amelia Bloomer was a quiet participant of the Seneca Falls women's convention in 1848, which was called by Lucretia Mott and Elizabeth Cady Stanton. Soon after the convention, she started a newspaper called *The Lily*, which was devoted to women's rights and the cause of temperance. It was the first newspaper in America to be edited entirely by a woman.

In 1853 she began wearing full-cut pantaloons called "Turkish trousers" under her skirt as an effort to liberate women from the heavy petticoats and cumbersome dresses that were required wear. She provoked a good deal of outrage and ridicule among men and conventional women. The outfit came to be known as "bloomers" because of her strong efforts to popularize the style. The style didn't last long but it was an attention-getter. Amelia remained a writer and lecturer for reform the remainder of her life.

 Reading Passages

Women's Suffrage *(cont.)*

Lucy Stone (1818–1893)

Lucy Stone was born in Massachusetts and at age 16 was earning a living as a poorly paid teacher. She attended several academies for girls and, in 1843, at the age of 25, entered Oberlin College, the only college open to women at the time. She gave public speeches opposing slavery and supporting women's rights, sometimes irritating abolitionist men. She called her own women's rights convention in Worcester, Massachusetts in 1850, and drew a lot of attention from the press.

Lucy married Henry Blackwell, brother to Elizabeth and Emily (who would both become doctors) when she was 36 years old, despite her earlier resolution never to marry. The marriage ceremony included a protest against existing marriage laws, and Lucy refused to take her husband's name, becoming the first woman to keep her maiden name.

Lucy Stone remained involved in various suffrage activities throughout her life. She and more conservative followers split from Susan B. Anthony and Elizabeth Cady Stanton in 1869 because Stanton and Anthony wanted to push for a broad range of reforms while Stone and her followers focused on the suffrage issue. In 1870 Stone founded the *Women's Journal*, a popular and long-lasting publication, to promote suffrage. The suffrage movement reunited in 1890. Lucy Stone gave speeches for the cause until her death in 1893.

Lucretia Mott (1793–1880)

Lucretia Mott was a Quaker schoolteacher and minister who became involved in many issues of social reform including the abolition of slavery, peace, and temperance. She helped create the American Anti-Slavery Society and the Anti-Slavery Convention of American Women. In 1838 her home in Philadelphia was nearly burned by a mob angry about the anti-slavery convention. She and Elizabeth Cady Stanton called the first convention of women at Seneca Falls advocating equal treatment of women before the law and the right to vote. Her home became a station on the Underground Railroad after the passage of the Fugitive Slave Law in 1850. After the Civil War, Lucretia worked for educational opportunities for freed blacks and continued to speak eloquently for peace and women's rights.

Reading Passages

Women's Suffrage (cont.)

Carrie Chapman Catt (1859–1947)

Carrie Chapman was born in Wisconsin and grew up in Iowa. She worked her way through Iowa State College and became a principal in Mason City, Iowa in 1881. Two years later she was appointed superintendent of schools, one of the first women in America to hold that position. She married Leo Chapman, a newspaper owner who died a year later. She became an organizer of a local suffrage movement in Iowa and, in 1890, married George Catt, who supported her work. Carrie worked for the National American Woman Suffrage Association for a decade and became its president in 1900, succeeding Susan B. Anthony.

Carrie founded an international suffrage association and joined with Jane Addams in efforts to form a women's peace organization. She worked with Susan B. Anthony and Elizabeth Cady Stanton as they were ending their careers. Carrie led the final push to achieve the right of women to vote. During World War I, she designed a "Winning Plan" to push the nation toward a constitutional amendment for women's suffrage. This strategy was directed at both federal and state officials during the war years. The involvement of women in the war effort helped finally push through the 19th Amendment in 1920. Carrie remained an important leader in forming the League of Women Voters, and she continued her efforts toward international peace and child labor reform.

Alice Paul (1885–1977)

Alice Paul was a highly educated graduate of Swarthmore College who received a Ph.D. from the University of Pennsylvania in 1912. She formed a militant National Woman's Party and was involved in fierce protests for women's suffrage. Alice even chained herself to the White House gates. As a result, she was jailed and went on a hunger strike. She was force fed to keep her from starving. After the passage of the 19th Amendment, she drafted the first Equal Rights Amendment introduced in Congress. She spent her life working for international peace and women's rights in the United States and abroad.

Other Suffragettes

Other committed suffragettes included the poet Julia Ward Howe, the Grimke sisters, Antoinette Blackwell, lawyer Belva Lockwood, presidential candidate Victoria Woodhull, and temperance advocate Frances Willard among many other capable and dedicated proponents.

Reading
Passages

Native Americans

Indian Rights

Native Americans in the 1800s were a people in limbo. Most Americans were unconcerned with the mistreatment they received, and they were often considered people standing in the way of progress. American Indians had virtually no legal rights and they were not even considered to be citizens of the United States. Two Native American women were especially determined to save their people from extinction, to raise the consciousness of Americans, and to achieve legal rights and full citizenship for their people.

Sarah Winnemucca (c. 1842–1891)

Sarah Winnemucca was born in Nevada. She was the granddaughter of Chief Winnemucca of the Paiute Indians. Her people were subjected to many abuses by whites. Sarah was buried alive by her mother when she was five years old to hide her from a marauding gang of whites. She was later expelled from a school because white parents didn't want their children attending school with Indians. She learned both English and Spanish and became a translator for government officials on the reservation where her people were forced to live.

Sarah personally rode into an enemy Indian camp, rescued her family, and helped end one Indian war. She went on a speaking tour trying to make Americans aware of the mistreatment of Native Americans and even spoke to President Hayes. Sarah wrote the first book by a Native American woman author about the mistreatment of her people. She self-published her book *Life among the Piutes: their Wrongs and Claims* in 1883.

Susette La Flesche (c. 1854–1903)

Susette La Flesche was the daughter of the chief of the Omaha tribe in Nebraska. She was educated in Indian schools and a private school, and became a teacher on the Omaha reservation. In 1877 the U.S. government relocated the neighboring Ponca Indians to Oklahoma where many of the tribe got sick and died. The survivors left the reservation and returned to their native home, where they were captured and held at Fort Omaha.

Susette joined a sympathetic newspaper reporter named Thomas Tibbles and went on a speaking tour wearing her native costume and using her American Indian name, Bright Eyes. They did succeed in freeing the Poncas and crusaded for equal treatment for Native Americans and for their right to be legally treated as American citizens. Susette obtained the support of many important Americans which led to an act granting citizenship to U.S. Native Americans. Susette is remembered as the first Native American woman to publicly speak for Native American causes. She was honored in the Senate upon her death.

Native Americans *(cont.)*

Sacagawea (c. 1788 or 1790–1812 or 1884)

Sacagawea was a Shoshone Indian and the daughter of a chief. She was captured by Minitari Indians (also called Hidatsa) when she was about 12 years old. Tribes often raided other tribes for captives. She lived with the Minitari until she was sold as a wife to a French fur trapper named Charbonneau. Meriwether Lewis and William Clark hired Charbonneau to accompany them as an interpreter on their journey across the Louisiana Purchase. They particularly wanted Sacagawea to accompany them although she had just had a baby. She was a Shoshone, and they desperately needed to trade for horses with the Shoshone to help them cross the Bitterroot Mountains.

Sacagawea carried her baby the entire journey. She was invaluable in dealing with the Shoshone Indians and did help Lewis and Clark get horses. On one occasion, she became so sick that it seemed likely she would die, but Lewis treated her with herbs that she recognized, and she survived. On the Columbia River, her boat overturned. The cradle she often used to carry her baby was washed away, but she saved the men's invaluable journals from being lost. She probably died at Fort Manuel in 1812, but some believe she lived much longer.

The Lewis and Clark expedition might well have failed or been lost entirely without Sacagawea's knowledge and assistance.

Wilma Mankiller (1945–present)

Wilma Mankiller was born on a Cherokee reservation in Oklahoma on a farm with neither running water nor electricity and very poor soil. Her family was forced to relocate to an urban area where her father became a warehouse worker and union activist. After an unhappy marriage and an education as a social worker, Wilma became involved in the American Native Rights movement and then returned to Cherokee land in Oklahoma, where she built a home for her two daughters.

Wilma became involved in several self-help community-planning programs to improve housing, water systems, social services, and farming techniques. She was a skilled grant writer and very successful in getting funding for Cherokee projects. She was elected deputy chief and, in 1985, became Principle Chief of the Cherokee Nation, the first woman to ever serve as chief of a Native American tribe, although the Cherokee and several other tribes had a tradition of female leadership and involvement in selecting chiefs. She continued efforts to improve community health care, educational opportunities, job training, and economic growth. Wilma was reelected to a second term and became an important representative for Native Americans with government officials and Washington politicians.

 Reading Passages

Reformers and Change Makers

These women embraced very different methods of change. Some had radical methods and ideas. Others became the symbols of change.

Emma Willard (1787–1870)

Emma Hart had the outrageous idea for her time that even farm girls should be as well educated as boys. She was encouraged by her father to keep up her schooling and was soon teaching and a principal at an academy. She married Dr. John Willard, a man almost 30 years older than her. Emma studied her nephew's college textbooks and became determined to teach math, science, and the classics to young women. She opened a female seminary in 1814 in Middlebury, NY where she offered a very high level of education to girls. She wrote a pamphlet to the New York Legislature proposing a radical change in female education, an idea approved by former Presidents Jefferson and Adams.

Emma Willard tried to get the support of the state legislature for opening her Troy Female Seminary, but the all male legislators felt that women were incapable of learning math and the sciences. One even suggested teaching cows would do as much good! She eventually got some support from the community of Troy and opened Troy Female Seminary in 1821. It revolutionized the way women were taught and the curriculum they received. The students of her school became enormously influential in spreading her ideas throughout the nation. The private girl's school, now known as the Emma Willard School, is still in existence in Troy, New York.

Jane Addams (1860–1935)

Jane Addams, born to a well-to-do family, attended Rockford Female Seminary and tried medical school for a year. After a tour of Europe and a visit to a British settlement house for the poor, she settled into a run-down old mansion called Hull House in the middle of an immigrant slum in Chicago. Addams and other women from well-off families created a settlement house serving the needs of the urban and immigrant poor. They sponsored educational programs, vocational training, nursery care, and help for the immigrants in dealing with the many problems of slum life.

Jane Addams and her colleagues campaigned for better working conditions in factories, to outlaw child labor, to protect workers from dangerous chemicals, for tenement regulation, and other basic human rights for the underprivileged. She wrote several books promoting her concerns and the work at Hull House. Addams was a strong proponent of peace during World War I and worked on refugee relief during the war. In 1931 she was awarded the Nobel Prize for Peace, the first American woman to be so honored.

 Reading Passages

Reformers and Change Makers *(cont.)*

Victoria Claflin Woodhull (1838–1927)

Victoria Claflin Woodhull was one of the most eccentric and remarkable women in American history. The Claflin family was poor with 10 children and no regular income. When she was eight years old, Victoria and her sister, Tennessee, performed in her father's traveling medicine show where she went into trances and believed that she could communicate with the dead. At the age of 15, partly to escape her family, she married an older man, Dr. Canning Woodhull, who was an alcoholic. Victoria later divorced Woodhull but kept his name even after she married an attractive con artist named Colonel Blood.

In 1868, after several years of travel as fortune-tellers and healers, Victoria and Tennessee arrived in New York City where they met the recently-widowed Cornelius Vanderbilt, one of the richest men in the world. The attractive and personable girls offered to help him communicate with his dead wife and also offered him stock tips while they shared his mansion. One of Victoria's tips worked out, and they were instant millionaires.

In 1870 Vanderbilt helped them start their own stockbrokerage. They became the first women stockbrokers in America. Victoria's shrewd business sense made the company successful. Eventually 15 members of her family, including her dying former husband and Colonel Blood, lived with them in a fashionable New York mansion.

Using profits from the business, Victoria and Tennessee started their own weekly magazine supporting women's rights, tax reform, as well as promoting Victoria's decision to run for President of the United States on a party that she helped create called the Equal Rights Party. Victoria gave speeches to suffrage groups and obtained some support from Susan B. Anthony and Elizabeth Cady Stanton. Victoria even managed to address Congress and meet President Grant.

Some of her radical positions provoked a backlash, and Victoria was widely criticized for her lifestyle and past behavior. She used her magazine to attack her critics and published the details of an affair between the most respected minister in America, Henry Ward Beecher, and one of his parishioners. Woodhull was arrested for sending obscene material through the mail and was in jail on Election Day so that she couldn't even try to vote. Victoria was eventually acquitted of the charge and moved to England with her sister. Both girls married wealthy British citizens.

Reformers and Change Makers *(cont.)*

Belva Lockwood (1830–1917)

Belva Ann Bennett was born in central New York and was teaching school by the age of 15. After a brief marriage, she attended Genesee College and resumed teaching in her own private school in Washington, D.C. In 1868 she married Ezekiel Lockwood and tried to enter graduate school in several local universities with law schools but was refused admission because she was a woman. Eventually, Belva gained admittance. She graduated from the National University Law School in 1873 and was admitted to the Washington D.C. bar. Belva advocated reforms in government practice to provide women with equal protection under the law. She drafted a successful Congressional bill requiring equal pay for equal work for women in government service.

"Mistress Lockwood, you are a woman," Justice Drake told Belva in 1876, explaining the Supreme Court's refusal to let her practice before the highest court in the land. Belva spent the next three years lobbying a bill through Congress that would make it illegal to exclude an attorney from practice before the high court based on her sex. She became the first woman allowed to practice before the Supreme Court. Belva Lockwood then opened a mother-daughter law firm. Among their successes was a suit against the government by the Cherokee Nation for five million dollars.

Mrs. Lockwood gave speeches and worked with various suffrage organizations. In 1884 she decided to run for President of the United States as the candidate of the Equal Rights Party. After a serious campaign, she won over 4,000 votes. She ran again in 1888. In 1896 she was successful in a campaign to get equal property and child-custody rights for women in Washington, D.C. She continued her work for women's suffrage, world peace, and equal legal rights for the remainder of her life.

Jeannette Rankin (1880–1973)

Jeannette Rankin was born in Montana, graduated from the University of Montana, and studied social work at Columbia University in New York. She worked as a social worker in Seattle and campaigned for women's suffrage in California and Washington. In 1914 she led the successful campaign for women's suffrage in Montana. In 1916 Jeannette Rankin was elected as the first woman to serve in the United States House of Representatives and joined 48 other Congressmen in 1917 opposing U.S. entry into World War I. She was defeated for the U.S. Senate in 1918. Jeannette continued to work as a social worker and lobbyist for women's causes, and was elected to a second term as an independent to the House of Representatives in 1940. She was the only member of Congress in the House or Senate to vote against U.S. entry into World War II. She continued to work for peace, social justice, and feminist causes until her death.

18

Reformers and Change Makers (cont.)

Shirley Chisholm (1924–2005)

Shirley St. Hill was the daughter of immigrant parents from Guyana and Barbados. In 1949 she married Conrad Chisholm. She graduated from Brooklyn College and taught school in Brooklyn until she received a master's degree in elementary education from Columbia University in 1952. She became a director of a childcare center in Manhattan and a consultant to the New York City Bureau of Child Welfare. Shirley soon became politically involved in solving neighborhood and city problems. She was fluent in Spanish and popular with the predominantly poor and black citizens of her district. Unhappy with the sense of isolation and disenfranchisement her community felt, she decided to run for the State Assembly. In 1964 she won a seat as an independent Democrat in the New York State Assembly.

In 1968 Shirley Chisholm ran for Congress as a representative of her impoverished Bedford-Stuyvesant community in Brooklyn. She won and became the first African-American woman ever elected to Congress. Her 1970 book, *Unbought and Unbossed*, expressed her political independence. Shirley became an extremely effective and dynamic spokesperson for the needs of all minority citizens, for the poor, the disadvantaged, and especially for children. She was a vocal supporter for the rights of women and opposed the Vietnam War. Shirley Chisholm was reelected repeatedly until her retirement in 1982. In 1971 she was a founding member of the National Women's Political Caucus designed to bring more women into the political arena. She entered the Democratic presidential primaries in 1972 and received 151 votes at the convention. In retirement, she taught college for two years and was involved in community politics where she remained a powerful voice for the rights of the disadvantaged.

Sandra Day O'Connor (1930–present)

Sandra Day was born in Texas, grew up on a ranch in Arizona, and graduated from Stanford University in California with a law degree. She met her future husband, John O'Connor, while at Stanford. She worked in a district attorney's office in California, had her own practice in Arizona, was an Arizona assistant district attorney, and became a state senator. She became the majority leader in the Arizona State Senate, the first woman in the country to hold that job, and was appointed to the Arizona Court of Appeals. In 1981 President Reagan appointed her as the first woman justice on the United States Supreme Court, where she demonstrated a very independent mind and a moderate judicial philosophy for more than 25 years.

Other Reformers

Women have been at the forefront of the reform movement in America since colonial times. Carry A. Nation and Frances Willard led the Temperance Crusade against the abuses of alcohol. Mary MacLeod Bethune, daughter of slaves, started a school and then a college to provide opportunities for young black women. Fannie Lou Hamer was a civil rights leader, freedom marcher, and voter registration activist.

Reading Passages

Scientists and Astronauts

American women have made significant contributions in many fields of science and they have become very important leaders in the exploration of space.

Maria Mitchell (1818–1889)

Maria Mitchell was born on the island of Nantucket in Massachusetts. She attended schools on the island and became very interested in studying the stars, a pursuit encouraged by her father. By the time she was 16, Maria had worked as a teacher and opened her own school. Later, she worked in a local library during the day so that she could study the sky at night. In 1846 Maria discovered the orbit of an unknown comet. The discovery earned her respect in the European and American scientific communities.

Maria became the first woman elected to the American Academy of Arts and Sciences in 1848. Years later, a group of civic-minded American women gave her a large telescope to use in her studies. Maria became the director of the observatory and a popular and influential professor of astronomy at the newly created Vassar Female College in 1865. She studied the planets with her students for 23 years before she retired in 1888.

Margaret Mead (1901–1978)

Margaret Mead was born in Philadelphia and graduated with her Ph.D. degree in anthropology from Columbia University in 1929. She made a celebrated trip to Samoa in 1925 where she spent two years observing the development of native children and adolescents. She published *Coming of Age in Samoa* in 1928, a book that challenged American concepts about child rearing and which introduced the science of cultural anthropology to a wider audience.

In later works, Margaret contrasted growth and development among several primitive societies in New Guinea and the western Pacific, as well as among Native Americans. She also wrote books on American culture, cultural changes in societies, and sexual development. She became a widely read and highly respected social critic. Mead worked at several universities and was associated with national and international societies devoted to mental health, science, and anthropology.

Reading Passages

Scientists and Astronauts *(cont.)*

Grace Murray Hopper (1906–1992)

Grace Murray was born in New York City and strongly encouraged by her parents to acquire an education. She graduated from Vassar College and obtained her Ph.D. in math from Yale University in the 1930s. She married Vincent Hopper in 1930, but different interests led to a divorce in 1945. She taught math at Vassar until World War II when she volunteered for the WAVES, women commissioned as officers by the Navy. She worked for the Navy at Harvard University on a Mark I computer, the earliest type of computer. The work involved determining exact firing trajectories for large guns on ships. She once found a moth interrupting the flow of information in a computer. She is said to have coined the term "bug" to describe the faulty operation of a computer.

After the war, Grace worked at Harvard developing the first compiler, a device which translates instructions into short codes which a computer reads. She helped develop COBAL, a widely used simplified computer language using English commands. Grace retired from the Navy Reserve in 1966, but returned to active duty to oversee the coordination of Navy computer systems. She became the first woman rear admiral in the Navy before her retirement in 1986 after 43 years of service. Grace Hopper wrote more than 50 articles about computing and was considered to have a problem-solving mind and a blunt style.

Rachel Carson (1907–1964)

Rachel Carson was born in Pennsylvania and attended the Pennsylvania College for Women with a major in biology. She received an M.A. in biology from Johns Hopkins University and taught for five years at the University of Maryland. She became an aquatic biologist for the U.S. Bureau of Fisheries from 1936 until 1952 where she used her writing skills and scientific knowledge in government publications and fieldwork. She wrote her first book in 1941. Carson's second book, *The Sea Around Us*, became a best seller in 1951. She published *The Edge of the Sea* in 1955.

Carson provoked a stream of controversy with her last book, *Silent Spring*, published in 1962. This best seller took on the issue of the agricultural use of pesticides and herbicides. She catalogued the misuse of these chemicals and the effects they had on humans and on ecosystems. The book provoked a storm of controversy and was widely criticized by agriculture and chemical companies, which had a vested interest in the products. President Kennedy read the book and supported its conclusions. Rachel didn't live to see the governmental controls imposed on the use of these chemicals before she died of cancer.

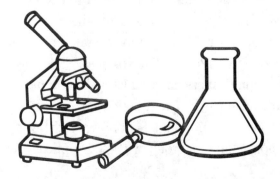

Reading Passages

Scientists and Astronauts *(cont.)*

Sally Ride (1951–present)

Sally Ride was born in Los Angeles, California, where she was a high school tennis star. She graduated with degrees in English and physics from Stanford University. Sally received her Ph.D. in physics at Stanford and entered the astronaut program in 1978. She became a Shuttle Mission Specialist and was the first American woman to fly into space in June of 1983. Sally Ride made a second space flight in 1984. Her scheduled third flight was canceled because of the *Challenger* explosion in 1986. She worked on the presidential commission appointed to determine the cause of the disaster. Later, she worked on strategic planning for NASA and in 1987 returned to Stanford as an instructor. She became a professor of physics and head of the Space Science Institute at UC San Diego in 1987. Sally Ride spent 337 hours in space. She is an author and travels the country speaking at science-based conferences.

Christa McAuliffe (1948-1986)

Christa McAuliffe was the first teacher and the first private citizen to go into space. She graduated from Farmington State College in Massachusetts and received an M.A. in education from Bowie State College in Maryland. Married and the mother of two children, Christa taught in several junior high and high schools in the Northeast. She was teaching American law, history, economics, and a course on The American Woman at Concord Senior High School when she was chosen out of a group of 10,000 applicants to be the first teacher in space.

Christa went through rigorous training for the mission and planned to do science experiments on board the shuttle. She kept a record of her training and activities for the time after her flight when she would travel throughout the nation promoting the importance of teachers, technology, and space exploration. After several delays, the *Challenger* was launched on January 28, 1986. It exploded 73 seconds into the flight while millions watched on television. An inquiry into the explosion pointed out serious flaws in NASA's safety record and delayed future missions for two years. Christa's influence helped make spaceflight a goal for many young women.

Mae Jemison (1956–present)

Mae Jemison is a brilliant doctor who became the first African-American woman to go into space. She has a degree in chemical engineering and strong interests in art, dance, and theater. She received a medical degree from Cornell University and served in the Peace Corps in West Africa and with the National Institutes of Health on several research projects aimed at the treatment of infectious diseases. Mae completed her astronaut training in 1988 and made her maiden space flight in 1992.

Dr. Jemison left NASA in 1993 and went on to teach at Dartmouth. She also established the Jemison Group, a firm that researches, develops, and markets advanced technologies.

 Reading Passages

Pioneers in Medicine

Some of the most important contributions to modern medicine have come from American women who recognized the need for better medical treatment of wounded soldiers, identified serious health dangers in factories, and pioneered more effective care for women and children.

Dorothea Dix (1802–1887)

Dorothea Dix was teaching school by the age of 14, using a curriculum based on the natural sciences that she devised herself. At age 19, she opened her own school in Boston where she taught for many years. At 22, she wrote one of the earliest science texts for children. After a serious bout of tuberculosis, Dorothea started teaching Sunday school in 1841 in a Massachusetts prison.

She was appalled at the treatment of the insane and mentally disturbed who were thrown in with dangerous criminals regardless of their gender. The mentally ill were often severely whipped and chained to walls. They were left unclothed, barely fed, and without any sanitation facilities. Dorothea traveled for two years throughout Massachusetts observing the treatment of these unfortunates. She submitted a report to the Massachusetts legislature that led to the creation of a treatment facility for the mentally ill.

For the next 40 years, Dorothea Dix campaigned in 15 states and Canada for the rights of the mentally ill and succeeded in getting 32 hospitals for the insane built. She also pressed for the general reform of prisons. In 1861 President Lincoln appointed Dorothea Dix as superintendent of nurses for the Union Army. She irritated many officers but saved thousands of lives with her insistence upon proper treatment and sanitation for wounded soldiers.

Clara Barton (1821–1912)

Born in Massachusetts, Clara Barton became a successful school teacher and established her own free school in Bordentown, New Jersey, which she ran until the town insisted upon a male principal. She left the school and soon went to work as a clerk for the U.S. Patent Office. When the Civil War began, Clara became a volunteer nurse for wounded soldiers and then expanded her efforts to bring supplies and other volunteers right onto the battlefields. Eventually, Barton took charge of some Union hospitals and became a superintendent of nurses for one Union Army. The soldiers called her "the angel of the battlefield."

After the war, she organized efforts to search for soldiers who were missing in action or who died in military prisons like the notorious Andersonville Prison. In 1881 she founded the American Red Cross to help in wars and natural disasters. She served as its president until 1904.

Reading Passages

Pioneers in Medicine *(cont.)*

Alice Hamilton (1869–1970)

Alice Hamilton was born into a well-to-do family and was homeschooled in Latin, German, French, literature, history, and math. Alice entered one of the few universities which would accept women in its medical program, the University of Michigan. After graduation, she worked as a physician serving poor people in Boston and did graduate work in Germany and at Johns Hopkins University in Baltimore. She became a professor at Northwestern University in Chicago and lived at Hull House, a settlement house for the poor founded by Jane Addams.

Alice became deeply concerned about the illnesses suffered by poor and immigrant factory workers and soon realized that many workers were suffering from lead poisoning and illnesses created by other chemicals. She worked on commissions to create safer working environments for all workers and lobbied for stricter state and federal laws regulating the use of chemicals in the workplace. Hamilton discovered that the use of some chemicals caused diseases such as tuberculosis, poisoning from breathing solvents, and insanity. She was the first female medical doctor on the faculty of Harvard University and spent the rest of her long lifetime studying, writing, and working to combat factory-related health problems.

Mary Edwards Walker (1832–1919)

Mary Edwards Walker was born on a farm in New York and graduated from Syracuse Medical College in 1855. She practiced medicine with her physician husband until they separated in 1859. She worked as a volunteer nurse in the U.S. Patent Office Hospital until she was appointed assistant surgeon in the Army of the Cumberland. She was the only female surgeon during the Civil War. She also worked in a women's prison and an orphanage during the war.

Mary was a strong advocate of "bloomers" before the war and adopted her own version of a male surgeon's uniform during the war. She was president of the National Dress Reform Movement and was often arrested for wearing men's clothes. She worked with Belva Lockwood in a variety of reform efforts. Mary was awarded the Congressional Medal of Honor for her work during the war, but it was later revoked.

Reading Passages

Pioneers in Medicine *(cont.)*

Elizabeth Blackwell (1821–1910)

Elizabeth Blackwell emigrated from England to America with her family when she was 11 years old. Her father had been a successful businessman, but his sugar refinery burned down and his last business venture was in debt when he died. Elizabeth gave piano lessons and taught school to help her family and began to study medical books and medicine with local doctors. There were no women doctors in America. She applied to 29 medical schools, but each turned her down.

Elizabeth was eventually accepted by the Geneva College of Medicine in Geneva, New York, because she had a recommendation from a renowned Philadelphia doctor. The administration stipulated that all 129 male students had to vote on her acceptance, expecting them to refuse to accept her. Unwilling to do the administration's dirty work, the boys voted unanimously to accept her. Despite the opposition of some instructors and a few students, she was soon recognized as the best student and graduated first in her class. She became the first woman doctor of modern times. Elizabeth received further training in England and France where she lost the use of her left eye when it was infected while she was caring for a baby. Her left eye had to be removed and replaced with a glass eye. As a result, she was not able to practice surgery.

Elizabeth Blackwell returned to the United States, but she was unable to find work in any hospital because she was a woman. She opened her own infirmary for women and

children in a slum district in New York City. She later expanded the infirmary and was joined by her sister, who was also a doctor, and a third woman doctor. By this time, some medical schools were accepting a few women candidates. Elizabeth helped organize associations for treating soldiers and trained nurses during the Civil War (1861–1865). Later, she opened the Women's Medical College at her infirmary. In 1869 she moved to England permanently, taught at the London School of Medicine, and wrote several books.

 Reading Passages

Pioneers in Medicine *(cont.)*

Emily Blackwell (1826–1910)

Determined to follow her older sister into medicine, Emily read medical books and applied to several medical colleges, including the Geneva College of Medicine which her sister had attended, only to be turned down. She was forced out of one medical college in Chicago due to community pressure on the school but finally graduated from the medical college at Western Reserve University in Cleveland.

Emily joined her sister at her New York City Infirmary and soon took control of the operations of the infirmary. She helped expand the services to include in-home medical services, social work, and a training college for nurses. In 1868 she founded a college for doctors that accepted both genders on an equal basis. It later combined with the Cornell University Medical College.

Mary Ann Bickerdyke (1817–1901)

Born in Ohio, Mary Ann Ball was brought up by a variety of relatives and, at age 30, married Robert Bickerdyke who died just before the Civil War. She practiced a kind of herbal medicine to support herself. At the outbreak of the Civil War, Mary volunteered to assist with supplies and nursing at a makeshift army hospital in Illinois. She immediately insisted on cleaning the facility and cooked and cared for the wounded soldiers. She went to battlefields to collect the wounded and soon attached herself to General Grant's staff.

Mary accompanied his troops into battle and treated wounded soldiers in the field.

She often enraged officers, especially the incompetent ones. Several of the worst officers were relieved of their command because of her reports. She worked through most of the war on the front lines with Grant and later with General Sherman. When several officers complained to Sherman about her insistence on sanitary treatment of the wounded and her generally bossy nature, he replied, "There is nothing I can do. She outranks me." To the soldiers, "Mother Bickerdyke" outranked everybody.

 Reading Passages

Artists and Writers

The women who enriched America's literary, musical, and artistic heritage shared their visions of life, love, and liberty with very diverse styles of expression reflecting their personal opinions, deeply held beliefs, and life experiences.

Mary Cassatt (1844–1926)

Mary Cassatt was born near Pittsburgh, Pennsylvania, lived in Europe for five years during her childhood with her family, and attended the Pennsylvania Academy of Fine Arts in her late teens. In 1866 she returned to Europe to study and settled in France. Once established in France, Mary befriended the Impressionist painter Edgar Degas. She became interested in using bright colors, experimenting with the effects of light, and using different subjects for her artistic compositions. She was also influenced by Japanese art. Her favorite subjects were women and children, and her work was characterized by the use of delicate shades of color. Mary Cassatt exhibited with the Impressionists in their shows in the 1880s. She also influenced wealthy Americans to invest in Impressionist paintings.

Georgia O'Keeffe (1887–1986)

Georgia O'Keeffe was born in Wisconsin and brought up in Virginia. She studied art at the Art Institute of Chicago and under several artist-teachers. She taught art at various schools and colleges. Georgia's early works were abstract paintings, followed by precise scenes of New York City and enlarged depictions of flowers. In 1924 she married a well-known gallery owner who was greatly impressed by her work. In a 1929 visit to New Mexico, Georgia developed her now famous personal style characterized by bleak landscapes and stark desert scenes with prominent skulls. With her unique artistic style, Georgia was the first woman to have her own exhibit at New York's Museum of Modern Art.

Anna Mary "Grandma" Moses (1860–1961)

Anna Robertson was born on a farm in New York State, had little schooling, and started working as a hired girl at the age of 13. She married Thomas Moses and they bought a farm in New York in 1905, where they lived the rest of their lives. Her husband died in 1927. In her late seventies Anna started working with oil paints when arthritis forced her to give up embroidery. She copied postcards and popular prints at first but soon developed her own style based on memories of her childhood. An art collector saw her paintings displayed in a country drug store, and her work was soon on display in prominent museums and galleries. Grandma Moses' style, called "American primitive," became very popular. She produced more than 2,000 paintings, usually done on cardboard or Masonite board. They were colorful, detailed, and portrayed country scenes such as making maple sugar, catching a Thanksgiving turkey, and the houses, tools, and animals of farm life. She was 101 when she died.

Reading Passages

Artists and Writers *(cont.)*

Marian Anderson (1897–1993)

"A voice like hers is heard only once in a hundred years!" exclaimed Arturo Toscanini, one of the greatest orchestra conductors of all time. The voice he was describing belonged to Marian Anderson, an African American singer from South Philadelphia who rose to the top of the classical music world despite intense racial discrimination. Marian started singing in her local church when she was six years old and soon learned to sing bass, alto, tenor, and soprano parts.

Her congregation raised money for her to study with a music teacher in her late teens. When she was 19, she was able to study with one of the great music teachers in the world. She worked with him for over 20 years. She performed in some American venues, but her greatest success came when she went to Europe to sing and learn the languages in which most operas were written. She built a reputation as a superb classical singer in Germany, Norway, Austria, England, and other countries.

On her return to the United States, she performed in several successful concerts. In Washington, D.C., she was refused permission to sing in Constitution Hall by the owners, the Daughters of the American Revolution, because of her race. Even the intervention of Eleanor Roosevelt had no effect. So she sang on the steps of the Lincoln Memorial and drew a crowd of 75,000. In 1955 Marian Anderson became the first African American to perform with the Metropolitan Opera Company in New York City. She retired from singing after a nationwide tour in 1965.

Maria Tallchief (1925–present)

Maria Tallchief was born on an Osage Indian reservation in Oklahoma and, as a young child, studied piano and dance in Los Angeles and Beverly Hills. She joined a ballet company directed by the famous George Ballanchine, whom she married in 1946. The next year she joined the dance group that later became the New York City Ballet. Maria is generally considered the most accomplished American-born ballerina and was the prima ballerina of the company in the 1950s. She has worked with a variety of ballet companies since her retirement from the New York City Ballet in 1965.

Reading Passages

Artists and Writers *(cont.)*

Phillis Wheatley (c. 1753–1784)

Phillis Wheatley was captured as a slave in Senegal, on the west coast of Africa, when she was eight years old. She endured the terrible journey across the ocean and the cruel treatment by the crew who threw her sick mother to the sharks during the voyage. Thin, frail, ill, and wearing only rags, Phillis was named for the ship that brought her to Boston. There she was purchased by Susannah Wheatley, wife of a wealthy tailor. The family recognized the young slave girl's hunger for knowledge, and she was soon reading and studying with their 18-year-old daughter who was also sickly. Within a year, Phillis had learned English, was reading the Bible, and starting to learn Latin and Greek.

At the age of 12, Phillis began to write poetry, and her first poem was published in 1770. She began to read her poetry to Boston leaders, including John Hancock. In 1773 she accompanied the Wheatley's older son

Nathaniel to London. Her first volume of poetry was published there because no American printer would publish a work by a slave girl. In London, Phillis met many important dignitaries, including Benjamin Franklin. The Wheatley's emancipated her after her return from England.

She wrote poetry before and during the American Revolution, eventually writing five poetry books. Phillis even wrote to General Washington and met him. She married a freed slave and had three children, all of whom died in infancy. Phillis died about the age of 31 alone and destitute. She is remembered as the first African American to publish a book of poetry.

Emily Dickinson (1830–1886)

Emily Dickinson was the daughter of a respected Massachusetts lawyer. She attended Amherst Academy and Mount Holyoke Female Seminary in her teens but then returned home and rarely left home again. She spent much of her time writing poetry with a unique style and cadence and very careful craftsmanship. Many of the poems dealt with the deeper meaning of life and others with imaginary boyfriends. A handful of her poems were published without her permission during her lifetime. After her death, her sister found neat packages with hundreds of her poems. Several volumes were printed, but it was almost 60 years before most of the 1,775 poems were published, and it became clear that Emily Dickinson was one of America's poetic geniuses.

Reading Passages

Artists and Writers *(cont.)*

Laura Ingalls Wilder (1867–1957)

Laura Ingalls was born on February 7, 1867, in a log cabin in the Wisconsin woods. A year after Laura's birth, the family moved to Missouri. They soon left for Kansas hoping to file a homestead on government land. Under the Homestead Act passed in 1862, a family that built a house and farmed 160 acres would own the land in five years. Unfortunately, the land Pa chose was on an Osage Indian Reservation, and they were forced to leave a year later. This is the site for *Little House on the Prairie.*

Laura Ingalls Wilder was in her sixties when she decided to tell the story of her pioneer childhood. A true child of the frontier, she had traveled with her family across much of mid-western America looking for fertile land and a brighter future. After her marriage to Almanzo Wilder, they moved to Missouri and settled on Rocky Ridge farm in the Ozark Mountains where they would live the rest of their lives. A gifted writer with a clear, simple style, Laura's eight *Little House* books detailing her pioneer childhood became immensely popular and have remained so for over seventy-five years. Laura died on February 10, 1957, at the age of 90.

Maya Angelou (1928–present)

Maya Angelou was born Marguerite Johnson in St. Louis, Missouri, and brought up by her grandmother in Arkansas. Maya graduated from high school in San Francisco at age 16 and soon became a single parent. She had a difficult time but learned to be a performer. Maya (a nickname given her by her brother) became a performer in the opera *Porgy and Bess.* She studied dance and acted on the stage and in two television mini-series about African culture. She has been a magazine editor in Africa and published her first book, *I Know Why the Caged Bird Sings*, in 1970. Maya has written plays, scripts for films, five autobiographies, several volumes of poetry, and in 1993 became the first African-American woman to recite her poem at a Presidential inauguration when President Clinton was sworn into office. Maya is a college professor, gives lectures and recitations to many audiences, and directs films. She has been married and divorced three times. In 2008 she received the Marian Anderson Award honoring her leadership and its benefit to humanity.

Reading
Passages

First Ladies

The men who have become President of the United States have varied enormously in character, ability, and intelligence. The women who have accompanied them to the White House are also remarkably diverse, especially in personality and temperament. Many first ladies tried to encourage their husbands to broaden their vision and listen to the needs of women in the nation.

Abigail Adams (1744–1818)

"I desire you would remember the ladies and be more generous and favorable to them than your ancestors! Do not put unlimited power into the hands of husbands . . . If particular care and attention is not paid to the ladies, we are determined to foment a rebellion, and will not hold ourselves bound by any laws in which we have no voice or representation." These words were written by Abigail Adams to her husband at the Continental Congress meeting in 1776 to draft the Declaration of Independence. She believed in her version of the separation of powers long before it became a part of the American constitution.

Abigail Adams had no opportunity for formal schooling since it was rarely available to girls at the time. She did read French, as well as English, and was a very skilled letter writer. During her husband's long absences from home, she carried on a continuous flow of letters offering shrewd and honest advice and encouragement to Adams in his various government duties in the United States and Europe. Abigail managed the family farm very successfully, raised five children, kept up on all local politics and news, and supported her husband's efforts to create a new nation. She did travel to Europe during her husband's duties as Commissioner in Paris and Minister to Great Britain. Abigail and John had a long, happy, and rewarding marriage marked by mutual respect for each other's intelligence.

Dolley Madison (1768–1849)

Dolley Payne was born and raised a Quaker, but after her marriage to James Madison, she rejected the simple ways and clothes of her heritage. She was an attractive 26-year-old widow when she married the 43-year-old bachelor James Madison. Several inches taller than her husband, she always referred to her husband as "my dear little Mr. Madison." Dolley was a popular woman who had already helped Thomas Jefferson and his daughter as hostess for White House affairs.

Mrs. Madison was a lively, cheerful hostess during her husband's presidency. She was especially admired for her courage during the War of 1812, when British troops burned Washington and the White House. Before she evacuated the White House and after her husband had already left, Dolley gathered up many priceless national treasures. These included a copy of the Declaration of Independence and a famous portrait of George Washington which she cut from its frame. After her husband's death in 1836, she returned to Washington and was an important social figure until her death.

Reading Passages

First Ladies *(cont.)*

Edith Wilson (1872–1961)

Edith Wilson came closer to being an acting President than any other First Lady. Woodrow Wilson's first wife died of a kidney ailment in 1914. His cousin, who worked as a White House hostess, introduced him to her widowed friend, Edith Bolling Galt, and they became friends. She was a good conversationalist and a great person with which to discuss ideas. They were married in December 1915. Woodrow Wilson led America into World War I and launched an effort to create a League of Nations to prevent future wars. He suffered a stroke with a year and a half left to go in his second term. Following the doctor's orders, Edith shielded her husband from all but the most essential tasks. Working with Colonel House, a trusted aide, she made most of the day-to-day decisions affecting the government. She simply did not inform the press of the seriousness of his condition. President and Mrs. Wilson retired in 1921 from public life. Mrs. Wilson went on to ride in President Kennedy's Innaugural Parade.

Eleanor Roosevelt (1884–1962)

Eleanor Roosevelt was her husband's eyes, ears, and legs. During the 12 years of Franklin Roosevelt's presidency, she traveled to thousands of places to observe public works projects, and to monitor the effects of social programs and the impact of the Great Depression on people's lives. She also attended political meetings with local officials. She inspected civil defense efforts early in World War II and visited virtually every major front during the war.

Eleanor Roosevelt's parents died in her childhood, and she grew up in her grandmother's home and in an English boarding school. She married Franklin Roosevelt, a distant cousin, when she was 20. Her father's older brother, President Theodore Roosevelt, gave away the bride. She had six children. One child died in infancy. Eleanor supported her husband in spite of difficult times in their personal lives. She continued to do so when he contracted polio, a disease that left him crippled for the rest of his life.

She supported him in his political efforts to be elected Governor of New York and President of the United States. Mrs. Roosevelt regularly met with reporters and gave speeches for the President at events he couldn't attend. She wrote regular newspaper articles and turned in her membership in the Daughters of the American Revolution in protest at their refusal to let a black woman, Marian Anderson, sing at their hall in Washington, D.C.

Eleanor had a long list of social and political causes which were important to her and which she used her influence with the President to advance. She supported efforts to improve working conditions for factory workers, sought laws to regulate child labor, was determined to reduce racial prejudice in all areas of American life, and worked to further the equality of women. She rode in an airplane with her friend Amelia Earhart to promote women's involvement in aviation. After her husband's death, she continued to work for international peace at the United Nations and to support her humanitarian ideals. Mrs. Roosevelt's active involvement during her husband's presidency led to greater visibility by many of her successors.

Reading
Passages

First Ladies (cont.)

Betty Ford (1918–present)

Betty Ford was a model for the modern first lady. She was the first divorced woman to marry a future president. She and her husband both enjoyed the social life in Washington, D.C. They were ardent dancers, friendly to all, and enjoyed a very close personal life. A mother of four with a strong interest in politics and the nation, Betty was not shy about discussing issues of national concern with her husband and often with the press. Betty was an ardent supporter of women's rights and worked for the passage of the Equal Rights Amendment to the Constitution, despite the opposition and complaints of some of her husband's Republican political supporters.

Mrs. Ford was also very open about her own personal problems. Less than a month after entering the White House, Betty Ford underwent surgery for breast cancer. Her openness about this serious issue helped bring the issue fully into the national consciousness and led to long-term concerted efforts to find effective treatments and an ultimate cure for this illness.

In 1978, while living in the White House, Betty Ford sought treatment for her addiction to alcohol and prescription medications. Her willingness to discuss her personal problems also helped bring these serious issues into the open and provoked serious discussion and attention to these widespread, but often hidden, personal and family problems. In 1982 she helped found the Betty Ford Center in Rancho Mirage, California, for the treatment of these personal issues. She and her husband also helped create a domestic violence center to address that serious national issue and supported other charities as well.

Other First Ladies

Sarah Polk worked with her husband on legislation, helped him write speeches, offered shrewd political advice, and helped him win support for his programs. Julia Grant wrote the first autobiography of a first lady to be published. Lucy Hayes, nicknamed "Lemonade Lucy," supported educational reform, women's rights, and temperance. Frances Cleveland married her 48-year-old husband when she was 21. It was the first White House wedding, and Frances helped polish some of her husband's manners while raising five children.

Lady Bird Johnson supported causes dear to her including the National Wildflower Research Center, which she founded in 1982. She was an early conservationist. Many of the women who accompanied their husbands to the White House highlighted issues important to women. Rosalynn Carter supported the Equal Rights Amendment, worked to make mental health treatment more accessible, and still supports her husband's many postpresidential humanitarian efforts. Nancy Reagan campaigned against drug abuse. Hillary Clinton followed her husband's career with election as a U.S. Senator, as a presidential candidate, and, in 2009, as Secretary of State.

Abolitionists Quiz

Directions: Read pages 7–9 about American women in the movement to abolish slavery. Answer these questions based on the information in the selection. Circle the correct answer for each question below.

1. Which abolitionist author wrote *Uncle Tom's Cabin*?
   a. Harriet Tubman
   b. Lucy Stone
   c. Harriet Beecher Stowe
   d. Sarah Grimke

2. Which abolitionist was born in the South in a slave-holding family?
   a. Harriet Beecher Stowe
   b. Harriet Tubman
   c. Angelina Grimke
   d. Sojourner Truth

3. Which woman established stations for the Underground Railroad and led more than 300 slaves to freedom?
   a. Sojourner Truth
   b. Sarah Grimke
   c. Elizabeth Cady Stanton
   d. Harriet Tubman

4. Which woman is famous for her "Ain't I a Woman?" speech?
   a. Sojourner Truth
   b. Sarah Grimke
   c. Angelina Grimke
   d. Lucy Stone

5. What religious group did the Grimke sisters join in their fight against slavery?
   a. Catholics
   b. Quakers
   c. Baptists
   d. Jews

6. Which of these women met President Abraham Lincoln?
   a. Harriet Beecher Stowe
   b. Sojourner Truth
   c. Frances Wright
   d. both A and B

7. For which reform were Lucretia Mott and Susan B. Anthony famous advocates?
   a. prison reform
   b. temperance
   c. abolition
   d. child labor

8. Where did Harriet Beecher Stowe get the ideas for her novel, *Uncle Tom's Cabin*?
   a. her husband
   b. newspaper articles
   c. fugitive slaves
   d. other books

9. What does the word *emancipation* mean?
   a. freed from slavery
   b. imprison
   c. wanted by the law
   d. runaway

10. Who helped freed blacks after the Civil War?
    a. Harriet Tubman
    b. Sarah Grimke
    c. Sojourner Truth
    d. both A and C

Women's Suffrage Quiz

Directions: Read pages 10–13 about leaders in the women's suffrage movement. Answer these questions based on the information in the selection. Circle the correct answer for each question below.

1. Which woman went on a hunger strike in jail to protest her arrest for chaining herself to the White House gates?
   a. Susan B. Anthony
   b. Jane Addams
   c. Elizabeth Cady Stanton
   d. Alice Paul

2. Whose father wished she had been a boy because she was so independent?
   a. Susan B. Anthony
   b. Lucretia Mott
   c. Carrie Chapman Catt
   d. Elizabeth Cady Stanton

3. Who designed the "Winning Plan" and led the final successful push for women's right to vote?
   a. Carrie Chapman Catt
   b. Susan B. Anthony
   c. Alice Paul
   d. Amelia Bloomer

4. Which woman was pictured on a U.S. dollar coin?
   a. Susan B. Anthony
   b. Amelia Bloomer
   c. Lucy Stone
   d. Lucretia Mott

5. Which was the first newspaper in the United States to be edited entirely by a woman?
   a. *Revolution*
   b. *New York Times*
   c. *The Lily*
   d. *Women's Journal*

6. What does *suffrage* mean?
   a. the right to drink
   b. equal property rights
   c. equal pay
   d. the right to vote

7. Which suffragette was also a Quaker minister, schoolteacher, and founder of an anti-slavery society for women?
   a. Carrie Chapman Catt
   b. Belva Lockwood
   c. Lucretia Mott
   d. Susan B. Anthony

8. Which of these things did Lucy Stone not do?
   a. attend college
   b. get married
   c. take her husband's name
   d. protest marriage laws

9. What was the *Declaration of Sentiments*?
   a. a greeting card
   b. a list of rights for women
   c. a wedding ceremony
   d. a newspaper article

10. Which amendment to the Constitution granted women the right to vote?
    a. 12th
    b. 19th
    c. 22nd
    d. 18th

Native Americans Quiz

Directions: Read pages 14–15 about Native American women. Answer these questions based on the information in the selection. Circle the correct answer for each question below.

1. Which Native American was crucial to the success of the Lewis and Clark expedition?
   a. Wilma Mankiller
   b. Susette La Flesche
   c. Sacagawea
   d. Sarah Winnemucca

2. Which Native American crusader for Indian rights was called Bright Eyes in her Omaha language?
   a. Sacagawea
   b. Wilma Mankiller
   c. Sarah Winnemucca
   d. Susette La Flesche

3. In which tribe was Wilma Mankiller the first Principle Chief?
   a. Ponca
   b. Omaha
   c. Cherokee
   d. Shoshone

4. Into which tribe was Sacagawea born?
   a. Minitari
   b. Shoshone
   c. Cherokee
   d. Hidatsa

5. Which of the following reforms for Native Americans did Susette La Flesche try to accomplish?
   a. land reform
   b. better education
   c. U.S. citizenship
   d. end to reservations

6. Who wrote the first book by a Native American woman?
   a. Wilma Mankiller
   b. Susette La Flesche
   c. Sacagawea
   d. Sarah Winnemucca

7. Which president did Sarah Winnemucca meet about Native American rights?
   a. Lincoln
   b. Hayes
   c. Cleveland
   d. Grant

8. What did Sacagawea save which was invaluable to Lewis and Clark?
   a. a boat
   b. her husband
   c. their journals
   d. several horses

9. Which of the following things were done by Sarah Winnemucca?
   a. rescued her family
   b. stopped a war
   c. became a chief
   d. both A and B

10. Which word means a place where Native Americans were forced to live after their native homelands were lost to settlers?
   a. expedition
   b. reservation
   c. fort
   d. survivor

Reformers and Change Makers Quiz

Directions: Read pages 16–19 about American women determined to reform society. Answer these questions based on the information in the selection. Circle the correct answer for each question below.

1. Who was the first woman to run for President of the United States?
   a. Shirley Chisholm
   b. Jeannette Rankin
   c. Victoria Claflin Woodhull
   d. Jane Addams

2. Which of the following social policies was not advocated by Jane Addams?
   a. abolition of slavery
   b. outlaw child labor
   c. international peace
   d. better working conditions

3. Who was the only member of Congress to vote against the United States' entry into both World War I and World War II?
   a. Jane Addams
   b. Jeannette Rankin
   c. Sandra Day O'Connor
   d. Carry A. Nation

4. Who wrote the book *Unbought and Unbound* to express her political independence?
   a. Jeannette Rankin
   b. Emma Willard
   c. Jane Addams
   d. Shirley Chisholm

5. Who was the first woman attorney to practice before the United States Supreme Court?
   a. Sandra Day O'Connor
   b. Victoria Woodhull
   c. Belva Lockwood
   d. Emma Willard

6. What institution did Emma Willard create?
   a. Hull House
   b. Troy Female Seminary
   c. Congress
   d. Vassar College

7. Who was the first female justice of the United States Supreme Court?
   a. Belva Lockwood
   b. Sandra Day O'Connor
   c. Victoria Woodhull
   d. Jane Addams

8. Which of the following did Victoria Claflin Woodhull not do?
   a. run for President
   b. communicate with the dead
   c. become a stockbroker
   d. start a school for girls

9. What is a "seminary for girls?"
   a. a government job
   b. an academy
   c. a type of clothing
   d. a religious group

10. Why was Belva Lockwood prohibited by Justice Drake from practicing before the Supreme Court?
    a. She was too old.
    b. She was a woman.
    c. She had no education.
    d. She was poorly dressed.

Scientists and Astronauts Quiz

Directions: Read pages 20–22 about American women scientists and astronauts. Answer these questions based on the information in the selection. Circle the correct answer for each question below.

1. Which of the following scientific occupations did Maria Mitchell pursue?
   a. astronaut
   b. astronomy
   c. anthropology
   d. biology

2. Which book was not written by Rachel Carson?
   a. *Silent Spring*
   b. *The Sea Around Us*
   c. *Coming of Age in Samoa*
   d. *The Edge of the Sea*

3. Which of these scientific accomplishments are credited to Grace Hopper?
   a. first woman in space
   b. discovered a comet
   c. developed computers
   d. studied native peoples

4. What does an anthropologist study?
   a. stars and planets
   b. human development
   c. motion
   d. living organisms

5. Which of these accomplishments is not credited to Mae Jemison?
   a. studied comets
   b. Peace Corps volunteer
   c. medical doctor
   d. first African-American female astronaut

6. What computer-related term did Grace Hopper invent?
   a. Internet
   b. web
   c. bug
   d. spam

7. How long did Sally Ride spend in space?
   a. 73 seconds
   b. 10,000 minutes
   c. 337 hours
   d. 43 years

8. Which of the following instruments would be in an observatory?
   a. microscope
   b. telescope
   c. stethoscope
   d. X-ray machine

9. Which of the following women did not travel into space?
   a. Maria Mitchell
   b. Mae Jemison
   c. Sally Ride
   d. Christa McAuliffe

10. What is a pesticide used for?
    a. to kill cattle
    b. to kill plants
    c. to kill germs
    d. to kill insects

Pioneers in Medicine Quiz

Directions: Read pages 23–26 about American women who were pioneers in medicine. Answer these questions based on the information in the selection. Circle the correct answer for each question below.

1. Who was the only female army surgeon the Civil War?
   a. Alice Hamilton
   b. Clara Barton
   c. Mary Edwards Walker
   d. Elizabeth Blackwell

2. Which woman campaigned to create institutions instead of prisons for the mentally ill?
   a. Elizabeth Blackwell
   b. Dorothea Dix
   c. Clara Barton
   d. Emily Blackwell

3. Who was known as the "angel of the battlefield"?
   a. Mary Edwards Walker
   b. Dorothea Dix
   c. Mary Ann Bickerdyke
   d. Clara Barton

4. What issue was Alice Hamilton most concerned with?
   a. treatment of soldiers
   b. the mentally ill
   c. health of factory workers
   d. medical education of women

5. Who did President Lincoln appoint superintendent of nurses for the Union Army?
   a. Mary Ann Bickerdyke
   b. Mary Edwards Walker
   c. Dorothea Dix
   d. Alice Hamilton

6. What does *sanitation* mean?
   a. cleanliness
   b. cannon fire
   c. insanity
   d. cruelty

7. Who wore "bloomers" and sometimes male clothes?
   a. Mary Edwards Walker
   b. Elizabeth Blackwell
   c. Dorothea Dix
   d. Clara Barton

8. Which of the following was a danger to personal health?
   a. lead poisoning
   b. tuberculosis
   c. chemical solvents
   d. all of the above

9. Who was the first woman doctor in the United States?
   a. Emily Blackwell
   b. Alice Hamilton
   c. Dorothea Dix
   d. Elizabeth Blackwell

10. Who said, "There is nothing I can do. She outranks me," about Mother Bickerdyke?
    a. Abraham Lincoln
    b. General Sherman
    c. General Grant
    d. Dorothea Dix

Artists and Writers Quiz

Directions: Read pages 27–30 about American women who were artists and writers. Answer these questions based on the information in the selection. Circle the correct answer for each question below.

1. Whose artistic style was called "American primitive"?
   a. Georgia O'Keeffe
   b. Grandma Moses
   c. Mary Cassatt
   d. Maria Tallchief

2. Which of the following is the most accurate description of Phillis Wheatley?
   a. painter
   b. singer
   c. author
   d. poet

3. Which of the following scenes is most characteristic of Georgia O'Keeffe's art?
   a. desert scenes
   b. farm scenes
   c. women and children
   d. medieval scenes

4. What is a *ballerina*?
   a. a writer
   b. a singer
   c. a dancer
   d. a sculptor

5. Why was Marian Anderson refused permission to sing in Constitution Hall?
   a. her singing style
   b. lack of money
   c. her political opinions
   d. her race

6. Who wrote *I Know Why the Caged Bird Sings*?
   a. Marian Anderson
   b. Laura Ingalls Wilder
   c. Maya Angelou
   d. Maria Tallchief

7. What is a *soprano*?
   a. a criminal
   b. a kind of poem
   c. a musical instrument
   d. a high singing voice

8. Which of the following women has been a playwright, a dancer, an actor, a poet, and a college professor?
   a. Maria Tallchief
   b. Maya Angelou
   c. Laura Ingalls Wilder
   d. Marian Anderson

9. Who wrote very complex poems but never chose to publish them in her lifetime?
   a. Emily Dickinson
   b. Phillis Wheatley
   c. Maya Angelou
   d. Mary Cassatt

10. Which of the following women was not a painter?
   a. Phillis Wheatley
   b. Mary Cassatt
   c. Grandma Moses
   d. Georgia O'Keeffe

First Ladies Quiz

Directions: Read pages 31–33 about America's first ladies. Answer these questions based on the information in the selection. Circle the correct answer for each question below.

1. Who told her husband to "Remember the ladies" in his work at the Continental Congress?
   a. Abigail Adams
   b. Eleanor Roosevelt
   c. Dolley Madison
   d. Edith Wilson

2. Who made day-to-day decisions running the government when her husband was ill with a stroke?
   a. Eleanor Roosevelt
   b. Sarah Polk
   c. Edith Wilson
   d. Dolley Madison

3. Which first lady rode with Amelia Earhart to promote women's involvement in aviation?
   a. Edith Wilson
   b. Eleanor Roosevelt
   c. Rosalynn Carter
   d. Hilary Clinton

4. Why did Eleanor Roosevelt serve as her husband's eyes, ears, and legs?
   a. She didn't need protection.
   b. He suffered from polio.
   c. He didn't like to travel.
   d. She needed something to do.

5. Which first lady helped bring the issue of breast cancer to the forefront?
   a. Rosalynn Carter
   b. Abigail Adams
   c. Edith Wilson
   d. Betty Ford

6. Which of these actions were done by Dolley Madison?
   a. White House hostess
   b. rescued White House valuables
   c. gave speeches
   d. both A and B

7. Which first lady married her cousin and was given away as a bride by her uncle who was President?
   a. Eleanor Roosevelt
   b. Dolley Madison
   c. Hillary Clinton
   d. Edith Wilson

8. Which of these facts is true of Edith Wilson?
   a. She lost three sons in war.
   b. She was married to two presidents.
   c. She made many of the day-to-day decisions for her husband, the President.
   d. She was declared insane.

9. Which first lady supported the Equal Rights Amendment and her husband's humanitarian efforts?
   a. Hilary Clinton
   b. Rosalynn Carter
   c. Eleanor Roosevelt
   d. Dolley Madison

10. Which of the following things did Abigail Adams do?
    a. run a farm
    b. write informative letters to her husband
    c. raise five children
    d. all of the above

Teacher Lesson Plans for Language Arts

Newspapers

Objective: Students will learn to apply their language arts skills in using newspapers and writing a school newspaper.

Materials: copies of Focus on Nellie Bly (page 45) and Working with Newspapers (page 46); newspapers

Procedure:

1. Reproduce and distribute Focus on Nellie Bly. Have students read the page independently or together as a class.
2. Distribute newspapers. Reproduce and distribute Working with Newspapers. Review the assignment. Have students search through the newspapers for the information requested.
3. Assign students to create a student newspaper using the directions on the bottom of page 46.

Assessment: Go over the activity page with the students and discuss what they found. Review and share student newspaper entries.

Magazines

Objective: Students will learn to apply their language arts skills in using magazines and writing editorials.

Materials: copies of Focus on Sarah Josepha Hale (page 47) and Write an Editorial (pages 48–49); magazines

Procedure:

1. Reproduce and distribute Focus on Sarah Josepha Hale. Have students read the top of the page independently or together as a class.
2. Distribute magazines. Review the assignment with the class and help students find and read the editorial pages and letters to the editor in the magazines.
3. Reproduce and distribute Write an Editorial.
4. Have students write a brief summary of a newspaper editorial or a letter to the editor.
5. Review the format of an editorial and a persuasive essay with the students. Help students choose a topic for an editorial from the list provided on page 48. Have students write their clusters on the planning sheet on page 49. Help students create powerful and interesting lead sentences for their editorials. Have students write the editorials.

Assessment: Have students share summaries of published editorials. Encourage students to share the final copies of their editorials with the class.

Teacher Lesson Plans for Language Arts *(cont.)*

Vocabulary

Objective: Students will expand their knowledge of words and terms associated with the reform movements of the 19th and 20th centuries.

Materials: copies of The Language of Reform (page 50) and Crossword Puzzle (page 51); dictionaries and/or copies of Glossary (page 95)

Procedure:

1. Reproduce and distribute The Language of Reform and the Glossary page, if appropriate. Review the words with students. Have students complete the page independently. They may want to refer to selected pages in the Reading Comprehension section of this book.

2. Reproduce and distribute Crossword Puzzle. Review the words with the students. Have students complete the page independently.

Assessment: Correct both vocabulary worksheets and review meanings of the words with the class.

Poetry

Objective: Students will develop skills in reading and understanding poetry.

Materials: copies of "Battle Hymn of the Republic" (page 52); "America the Beautiful" (page 53); Reading Poetry in Two Voices (page 54); Understanding the Elements of Poetry (pages 55–56); Poetry in Two Voices (page 57); copies of poems listed on page 57 (available in books and on the Internet)

Procedure:

1. Reproduce and distribute "Battle Hymn of the Republic," "America the Beautiful," and Reading Poetry in Two Voices. Have students review the vocabulary and rhyme in the poems.

2. Review the nature of poetry in two voices, stressing the importance of timing so that the two voices work in unison. You may wish to assign this activity to two capable students and have them demonstrate how to present a narrative poem.

3. Reproduce and distribute Understanding the Elements of Poetry. Review the rhyme and figurative language in "Battle Hymn of the Republic" and "America the Beautiful."

4. Reproduce and distribute Poetry in Two Voices. Have each student pair choose a poem from the lists of suggestions on page 57, or assign one. Tell them to divide it into two parts with a chorus, and allow students to practice it several days before presenting it to the class. Help them with unfamiliar words and terms.

Assessment: Have students present their poems to the entire class. Base the performance assessments on pacing, volume, expression, and focus of the participants.

Teacher Lesson Plans for Language Arts *(cont.)*

Literature

Objective: Students will read from and respond to literature in the form of diaries and biographies.

Materials: copies of Diaries (pages 58–59), Biographies of Extraordinary Women (page 60), Selected Biographies of Extraordinary American Women (page 61), and Write Your Autobiography (page 62); copies of some of the diaries listed on page 59 and some of the biographies listed on page 61

Procedure:

1. Reproduce and distribute Diaries. Assign the diaries. Have students complete the Diary Notes section and share responses. Have each student create and maintain a diary.

2. Reproduce and distribute Biographies of Extraordinary Women, and Selected Biographies of Extraordinary American Women. Assign students to read the biographies and complete the Discussion Starters on page 60. Conduct reading circles using student responses in the Discussion Starters. The readers' circles could be organized by the subject of the biography or by students who had similar interests.

3. Reproduce and distribute Write Your Autobiography. Encourage students to use the cluster for Let Me Introduce You to . . . before writing their final drafts. Explain the meaning of an epitaph, and have students create epitaphs for themselves.

Assessment: Use student activity pages, diaries, and biographies, as well as class discussions, to assess students' performance.

Readers' Theater

Objective: Students will learn to use their voices effectively in dramatic reading.

Materials: copies of Readers' Theater Notes (page 63) and Readers' Theater: Bloomer Girls (pages 64–70)

Procedure:

1. Reproduce and distribute Readers' Theater Notes. Review the basic concepts of Readers' Theater with the class.

2. Reproduce and distribute Readers' Theater: Bloomer Girls. Put students in small groups, and allow time over several days for them to practice reading the script together.

3. Schedule class performances, and have students share the prepared script.

4. Use the suggestions in the Extensions activity at the bottom of page 63 to allow students to write their own Readers' Theater. Assign topics to teams of students, or let them choose their own. Allow time for them to create and practice their scripts.

5. Schedule classroom performances of these scripts, or invite another class to view a production.

Assessment: Base performance assessments on pacing, volume, expression, and focus of the participants. Student-created scripts should demonstrate general writing skills, dramatic tension, and a good plot.

Focus on Nellie Bly (c. 1867–1922)

Elizabeth Cochran was born in Pennsylvania and attended boarding school for a few months, but the family's lack of finances forced her to drop out. She wrote a letter to the *Pittsburgh Dispatch* protesting an article in that newspaper. She insisted that women should be allowed to vote and work outside the house. The editor liked her writing so much he offered her a job and suggested that she use the pseudonym Nellie Bly.

Nellie wrote sympathetic articles about factory girls and life in the slums. She wrote such detailed accounts of the corruption in Mexico that she was expelled from the country. When she joined the *New York World*, Nellie faked a mental illness and was imprisoned in an insane asylum where she recorded the cruel mistreatment of inmates. Later, she was arrested on a fake charge of shoplifting and reported the brutal treatment of jail inmates. Bly exposed mistreatment in sweatshops and bribery in the New York legislature. Nellie Bly became the best-known woman journalist in America at the time.

In 1889, inspired by Jules Verne's recently published *Around the World in Eighty Days*, Bly began a trip around the world. She was trying to complete the trip in less than 80 days. Traveling by ship and railroad, on rickshaws and horses, and by many other means, she and her pet monkey made it in 72 days. Nellie temporarily retired after marriage to a wealthy man. She returned to journalism after his death. Her books include *Ten Days in a Mad House*, *Six Months in Mexico*, and *Around the World in Seventy-Two Days*.

Working with Newspapers

Assignment

1. Examine the sections of any newspaper.
2. Find and identify these sections of a newspaper.
3. Skim or read each section listed.
4. Tell what news each section of this paper contained.

Front Page—Top—the most important news of the day

_____

Below the Fold—Front Page—important news

_____

Local News—news about your city or town

_____

National and International News

_____

Business and Stock Market

_____

Editorial Page—opinions of editors and readers

_____

Obituary Notices—recent deaths

_____

Sports—local and national sports events

_____

Other—comics—new books

_____

Create a School Newspaper

Become a reporter for a school newspaper which the class can publish on a computer and copy for students. Report on the activities in one classroom.

1. Talk to several students and the teacher. Ask questions about field trips; books being read; science, art, and music activities; math concepts; P.E. games; and student's creative writing projects.
2. Take careful notes and spell names correctly.
3. Use quotes from the teacher and two or three students.
4. Write a final copy with good grammar, spelling, and punctuation.
5. Combine the class articles in a newspaper.

Focus on Sarah Josepha Hale (1788–1879)

Sarah J. Hale was arguably the most important American woman of the 1800s. Born in New Hampshire, she was educated by her mother and brother, a Dartmouth student who came home from college each day and taught her what he had learned. Women were not then allowed to attend college. After her husband died, Sarah supported her five children by writing poetry for local publications, including the children's classic, "Mary Had A Little Lamb." She wrote *Northwood*, the first novel by a woman in America, and became the first woman magazine editor in 1827.

When *Ladies Magazine* became *Godey's Lady's Book*, Sarah used it as a vehicle for promoting her personal crusades. Starting in 1846, she badgered six presidents over 17 years to proclaim an annual National Day of Thanksgiving. Abraham Lincoln finally accepted her suggestion in 1863, a few weeks after the Gettysburg Address was delivered. Mrs. Hale campaigned for more female teachers and for the right of women to serve on school boards even before women could vote.

Sarah helped found Vassar College for women and supported teaching colleges and nursing colleges for women. She campaigned for property rights for women and championed the right of women to use newly discovered anesthetics during childbirth at a time when such a use was opposed by many religious leaders. Her magazine was the arbiter of women's fashions and she introduced some of the best writers in America to her audience, including Edgar Allen Poe, Harriet Beecher Stowe, and Nathaniel Hawthorne.

Assignments

1. Choose an appropriate magazine.
2. Find and read its Table of Contents.
3. Read several feature articles.
4. On a separate paper, write a one or two paragraph summary of one feature article.
5. Read several department pieces. Look for editorial comments, letters to the editor, and other interesting expressions of opinion.
6. On a separate paper, write a one- or two-paragraph summary of one opinion expressed in a department piece.

Write an Editorial

Sarah Josepha Hale was one of many extraordinary American women who believed in the power of the pen to change their world. She wrote many editorials and essays supporting her views. Like many change makers, she was a persuasive writer who advocated her causes with clarity and passion.

Editorial Format

Write an editorial in the form of a persuasive essay on one of the suggested topics listed below or another subject about which you have strong opinions.

Your editorial should have at least four paragraphs organized like this:

1. An opening paragraph should clearly express your opinion and indicate why the subject is important to you.

2. The second paragraph should describe the evidence you have to support your opinion—this could include personal experiences, the opinions of experts, and careful reasoning.

3. The third paragraph should describe the arguments and evidence against your position and your response and reactions to these arguments.

4. The concluding paragraph should briefly restate your position and clearly draw together all the elements of your thinking.

Suggested Topics

- The most important woman in American history was _____.
- Should a woman be elected President of the United States?
- Should girls be allowed to play football in high school and college?
- Should women have been allowed to vote?
- Girls are better students than boys.
- Should the voting age be lowered to 12?
- Should the United States have gone to war in Iraq?
- Should some students receive preferential admissions to colleges because they come from poor families and schools?
- Science is more important than art.
- Should boys and girls attend separate classes?
- Should high school graduation depend on passing a state required test?
- Should the driving age be lowered to 14?
- The most important subject in school is _____.
- Should grades be abolished in school?
- The best book ever written is _____.
- Should uniforms be required in school?
- The greatest invention in the world was _____.
- The greatest U.S. President was _____.
- Should the atomic bomb have been used to end World War II?

Write an Editorial *(cont.)*

Pre-write

Do your pre-write planning or cluster here. Write down notes and ideas in the proper sections.

Title: _____

_____

Paragraph 1—Opening Paragraph

your opinion/importance of the subject

_____

_____

_____

Paragraph 2

the evidence that supports your opinion

_____

_____

_____

Paragraph 3

arguments against your position and your response to them

_____

_____

_____

Paragraph 4—Concluding Paragraph

briefly restate your opinion and summarize your thinking

_____

_____

_____

Writing the Lead

Every effective editorial needs a good lead. This is the first sentence or two of the editorial and should grab and hold the attention of the reader. The lead may state your position in clear terms. It may be funny, clever, or have an unusual twist. Try several different leads for your editorial.

_____

_____

_____

The Language of Reform

Word List

abolition	emancipation	seminary
abolitionist	freedom marcher	spiritualist
activists	insane asylums	suffrage
Amendment	legislature	suffragettes
candidate	Quaker	temperance
Convention	reformers	voters' rights

Directions: Choose terms from the list above to complete the sentences below. Use the glossary, a dictionary, or the comprehension pages in this book for help.

1. Susan B. Anthony and Elizabeth Cady Stanton were _____ who

   fought for women's _____, the right to vote.

2. Lucretia Mott and Antoinette Blackwell were _____ who wanted to change
   the nation's laws regarding slavery, women's rights, and alcohol abuse.

3. The passage of the 19th _____ allowed women the right to vote.

4. Victoria Woodhull was a _____ who believed that she could communicate

   with the dead. In 1872, she was a _____ for president of the United States.

5. Lucretia Mott was a _____ minister and active in many causes, including women's rights

   and the _____ of slavery. She believed in the _____ of all slaves.

6. Fannie Lou Hamer was a _____ who fought for

   _____.

7. Emma Willard opened a private school or _____ for teaching young women.

8. Carry Nation was an important leader in the _____
   movement to end the use, abuse, and sale of alcohol.

9. Dorothea Dix led the movement to improve the treatment of prisoners and helped create

   _____ for the mentally ill.

10. Lucretia Mott and Elizabeth Cady Stanton called a Women's Rights _____

    _____ to influence the public and the _____ to change the laws.

Crossword Puzzle

Directions: Complete the puzzle using the word list and the definitions below.

Word List

abolitionist	feminist	seminary
amendment	legislature	sojourn
custody	patent	suffragettes
emancipation	protest	tenements
equal	Quaker	

Across

1. a person strongly opposed to slavery
3. the freeing of slaves
7. to have the same rights
10. women who fought for the right to vote
11. to have legal control of
12. ownership rights to an invention
13. a private school for young women

Down

1. a change to a law or the Constitution
2. housing for the very poor
4. to organize against a law or condition
5. a member of a religious group opposed to slavery and war
6. to stay temporarily (v.)
8. a group of lawmakers in a state or country
9. a leader for women's rights

"Battle Hymn of the Republic"

"Battle Hymn of the Republic" was originally written by Julia Ward Howe as a poem and published in the *Atlantic Monthly* magazine. It was later set to music using an old folk tune and became the symbolic song of the Union Army. Julia Ward Howe, a little known writer and abolitionist, became famous with the success of the song. She spent her years after the Civil War working for women's suffrage and international peace.

First Speaker   **"Battle Hymn of the Republic"** by Julia Ward Howe

Second Speaker
Mine eyes have seen the glory
of the coming of the Lord;
He is trampling out the vintage
where the grapes of wrath are stored;
He hath loosed the fateful lightning
of His terrible swift sword:

Chorus   His truth is marching on.

First Speaker
I have seen Him in the watch-fires
of a hundred circling camps;
They have builded Him an altar
in the evening dews and damps;
I can read His righteous sentence
by the dim and flaring lamps;

Chorus   His day is marching on.

Second Speaker
I have read a fiery gospel,
writ in burnished rows of steel:
"As ye deal with My contemners,
so with you My grace shall deal;
Let the Hero, born of woman,
crush the serpent with His heel,

Chorus   Since God is marching on.

First Speaker
He has sounded forth the trumpet
that shall never call retreat;
He is sifting out the hearts of men
before His judgment-seat;
Oh, be swift, my soul, to answer Him!
be jubilant, my feet!

Chorus   Our God is marching on.

Second Speaker
In the beauty of the lilies
Christ was born across the sea,
With a glory in His bosom
that transfigures you and me:
As He died to make men holy,
let us die to make men free,

Chorus   While God is marching on.

"America the Beautiful"

Katharine Lee Bates was a professor of English at Wellesley College in Massachusetts for 40 years and an author of volumes of poetry, travel, and studies of English literary works. In 1893, during a tour of the west where she climbed Pike's Peak, Katherine was so inspired by the sights that she wrote the poem, "America the Beautiful." It was published in a religious magazine in 1895. After several revisions, the poem was set to music and became America's most popular national hymn.

First Speaker

"America the Beautiful"
by
Katharine Lee Bates

Second Speaker

O beautiful for spacious skies,
For amber waves of grain,
For purple mountain majesties
Above the fruited plain!

Chorus

America! America!
God shed His grace on thee
And crown thy good with brotherhood
From sea to shining sea!

First Speaker

O beautiful for pilgrim feet,
Whose stern, impassioned stress
A thoroughfare for freedom beat
Across the wilderness!

Chorus

America! America!
God mend thine every flaw,
Confirm thy soul in self-control,
Thy liberty in law!

Second Speaker

O beautiful for heroes proved
In liberating strife,
Who more than self their country loved,
And mercy more than life!

Chorus

America! America!
May God thy gold refine,
Till all success be nobleness
And every gain divine!

First Speaker

O beautiful for patriot dream
That sees beyond the years
Thine alabaster cities gleam
Undimmed by human tears!

Chorus

America! America!
God shed His grace on thee,
And crown thy good with brotherhood
From sea to shining sea!

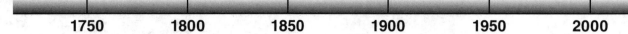
Reading Poetry in Two Voices

Directions

1. The "Battle Hymn of the Republic" on page 52 and "America the Beautiful" on page 53 are arranged to be read by two readers.

2. Choose a partner and the poem you will read together.

3. Read the poem silently several times.

4. Check the meanings of the italicized words in the Poetry Notes section below.

5. Decide who will be the first and who will be the second reader.

6. Read the chorus parts together.

7. Practice reading your poem several times over the course of a week or more.

8 Present your reading to the class and in other classrooms.

═══ Poetry Notes ═══

Poetic Words and Phrases—"The Battle Hymn of the Republic"

　　trampling–walking, as some wine makers do, on grapes

　　vintage–wine

　　grapes of wrath–fruits of fierce anger

　　hath–has

　　loosed–set free

　　fateful–fatal, mortal

　　terrible swift sword–an all-powerful weapon

　　the watchfires of a hundred circling camps–the campfires of the Union soldiers

　　builded Him an altar–built an altar (the campfires)

　　read His righteous sentence–see the decision of the Lord as judge of human actions

　　dim and flaring lamps–campfires and lanterns

　　fiery gospel–the word of God

　　writ in burnished rows of steel–expressed with shining swords and rifles

　　ye–you

　　My contemners–those who despised Christ

　　Hero, born of woman–Christ

　　crush the serpent with His heel–step on/kill the devil

　　sifting out the hearts of men–examining the men's motives

　　jubilant–joyful

　　a glory in His bosom that transfigures you and me–God changes the hearts of people

Poetic Words—"America the Beautiful"

　　amber–brown

　　thy–your

　　thine–your

　　divine–proceeding from God

　　alabaster–white-colored stone

Understanding the Elements of Poetry

"Battle Hymn of the Republic"

Rhyme

Poets used *rhyming words* at the end of lines of poetry to achieve a pleasing effect and to highlight some aspect of the poem such as the military beat in this poem. Sometimes the rhymes sound the same (vocal rhymes) and other times the rhymes were visual rhymes, meaning that they look like they rhyme.

1. List the rhyming words at the end of the lines in each stanza.

   1st stanza _____   _____   _____

   2nd stanza _____   _____   _____

   3rd stanza _____   _____   _____

   4th stanza _____   _____   _____

   5th stanza _____   _____   _____

2. What pattern can you find?

   _____

   _____

3. Does every end word in a stanza have a rhyming partner?

   _____

   _____

Figurative Language

Poets use figurative language to paint word pictures for the reader and the listener. Four types of figurative language are *personification*, *metaphor*, *simile*, and *hyperbole*.

Personification

Personification is a technique used to make something which is not human act or feel like a person.
"He is trampling out the vintage where the grapes of wrath are stored;"
God is spoken of as if he were a wine maker trampling on grapes.

Metaphor

A *metaphor* is a figurative comparison in which one thing is spoken of as if it were another.
"I have read a fiery gospel, writ in burnished rows of steel:"
The weapons of war are compared to a religious book.

Simile

A *simile* is a comparison of two different things using the words *like* or *as*.
"As He died to make men holy, let us die to make men free,"
The mission of the Union soldiers is compared to the salvation mission of Christ in the Christian religion.

Hyperbole

A *hyperbole* is a poetic exaggeration used to make a point.
"He hath loosed the fateful lightning of His terrible swift sword:"
God is portrayed using an all-powerful sword to defeat the enemy.
This hyperbole is also a metaphor comparing God to a warrior.

Understanding the Elements of Poetry *(cont.)*

"Battle Hymn of the Republic" *(cont.)*

Assignment

Find these three metaphors in the poem, "Battle Hymn of the Republic." Then tell what each metaphor is comparing.

1. Verse: "They have builded..." _____

   _____

   is compared to _____

   _____

2. Verse: "He is trampling..." _____

   _____

   is compared to _____

   _____

Simile

Finish this simile in the poem and then explain its meaning.

"As ye deal with My contemners..." _____

_____

is comparing _____

_____

"America the Beautiful"

Write the rhyming words from each stanza.

1st Stanza   _____   _____

                  _____   _____

Chorus   _____   _____

2nd Stanza   _____   _____

                  _____   _____

Chorus   _____   _____

3rd Stanza   _____   _____

                  _____   _____

Chorus   _____   _____

4th Stanza   _____   _____

                  _____   _____

Chorus   _____   _____

Poetry in Two Voices

Reading poetry aloud with a friend is a special way to enjoy poetry. In this type of presentation, two or more students recite a poem together. You and your partner will recite alternate verses or stanzas throughout the poem. You will read some sections together as a choral reading. Use "The Battle Hymn of the Republic" (page 52) and "America the Beautiful" (page 53) as samples for dividing your own poem. This technique can be used with any poem and some songs, but it is especially effective with ballads and story poems.

Assignment

- Choose a partner.
- Choose a poem from the selections listed below or others your teacher has provided. Pick a poem that appeals to you because of the rhyme, rhythm, or subject matter.
- Divide up the poem into parts so that you and your partner are reciting the poem back and forth together.
- Choose at least a few lines that both of you will recite together in chorus—out loud, at the same time.
- Copy your poem so that each of you has a copy to work with.
- Practice together so that you have the same speed, volume, and pace.
- Underline words which should receive special emphasis.
- Try to get a feel for the force and flow of the poetic language.
- Practice several times over the course of a week or more.
- Recite the poem for your class.

Suggested Poems by American Women

- "Travel" by Edna St. Vincent Millay
- "Departure" by Edna St. Vincent Millay
- "Song for the Old Ones" by Maya Angelou
- "Alone" by Maya Angelou
- "Human Family" by Maya Angelou
- "Our Country" by Julia Ward Howe
- "The New Colossus" by Emma Lazarus
- "Molly Pitcher" by Kate Brownlee Sherwood
- "The Brain is Wider then the Sky" by Emily Dickinson
- "Because I Could Not Stop for Death" by Emily Dickinson

Narrative Poems with American Settings

- "O Captain! My Captain!" by Walt Whitman
- "Paul Revere's Ride" by Henry Wadsworth Longfellow
- "Eldorado" by Edgar Allan Poe
- "John Henry" by Anonymous
- "Casey Jones" by Anonymous
- "Annabel Lee" by Edgar Allan Poe
- "The Cremation of Sam McGee" by Robert W. Service
- "Ode to Billy Joe" by Bobbie Gentry
- "The Bells" by Edgar Allan Poe
- "Casey at the Bat" by Ernest Lawrence Thayer

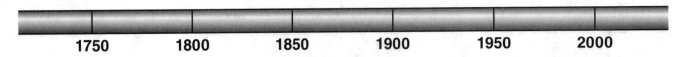

| 1750 | 1800 | 1850 | 1900 | 1950 | 2000 |

Diaries

Materials: Diaries reference page (page 59)

Assignment

Read one of the diaries listed on the Diaries reference page or one of the many other diaries in the *Dear America*, *My America*, *American Diaries*, and other diary series. Share your observations with your classmates or literature circle.

Diary Notes

Title of Diary: _____

Writer's Personal Data: age, personality, behavior, character traits, dreams, hopes, and desires _____

_____

Setting: historical time period and geographical area _____

_____

Problem/Conflict: people and events that affect her life _____

_____

Other Major Characters: friends, enemies, family members _____

_____

Important Events: happenings that affect the diarist's life _____

_____

Resolution: the end _____

_____

Impressions: your personal thoughts and feelings about the main character _____

_____

Questions: things you didn't understand _____

_____

Become a Diarist—Create Your Own Diary

1. Start your own diary or journal today! Don't put it off. Enjoy the creative expression.

2. Imagine that your children will someday read your diary or that it might be found by a researcher in the distant future or even that you will find your own diary when you are an adult.

3. Try to record at least one entry each day. Feel free to change your mind about people and events.

4. Describe the important events that are going on in your personal life. Be honest with yourself.

5. Record some of your daily habits and personal feelings about life.

6. Mention events in the world or your community which are affecting your life or may affect your life in the future.

7. Describe books you are reading that influence your thinking.

8. Mention your dreams, aspirations, and hopes for the future.

9. Describe important people in your life.

Diaries *(cont.)*

Many American girls and women of the past kept diaries. Some were famous, but many others were unknown. They recorded the adventures, experiences, and personal reflections of the lives they lived. The list below includes true diaries of girls and women and fictionalized diaries written to give the reader a sense of the many issues and historical events in our history.

Bunkers, Suzanne L. ed. *A Pioneer Farm Girl: The Diary of Sarah Gillespie, 1877–1878.* Blue Earth Books, 2000.
Life on the Iowa frontier seen from the eyes of a 13-year-old girl

Fraustino, Lisa. *I Walk in Dread: The Diary of Deliverance Trembley, Witness to the Salem Witch Trials.* Dear America Series, Scholastic, 2004.
Fascinating account of the events surrounding the trials

Janke, Katalan. *Survival in the Storm: The Dust Bowl Diary of Grace Edwards.* Dear America Series, Scholastic, 2002.
Dust Bowl life at school and at home in 1935 for a 12-year-old Texas farm girl and her family

Murphy, Jim. *West to a Land of Plenty: The Diary of Teresa Angelino Viscardi.* Dear America Series, Scholastic, 1998.
Realistic account of a teen enduring the dangers and deaths of the cross-country journey

O'Hara, Megan, ed. *A Colonial Quaker Girl: The Diary of Sally Wister, 1777–1778.* Blue Earth Books, 2000.
An interesting account of life for a girl in the midst of war

O'Hara, Megan, ed. *A Whaling Captain's Daughter: The Diary of Laura Jernegan, 1868–1871.* Blue Earth Books, 2000.
Three years on a whaling ship recorded by very young girl

Steele, Christy and Anne Todd, ed. *A Confederate Girl: The Diary of Carrie Berry, 1864.* Blue Earth Books, 2000.
Interesting diary of a Confederate girl in 1864

Steele, Christy and Ann Hodgson, ed. *A Covered Wagon Girl: The Diary of Sallie Hester, 1849–1850.* Blue Earth Books, 2000.
Life for a 14-year-old girl on the trek from Indiana to California

Steele, Christy and Kerry Graves, ed. *A Free Black Girl Before the Civil War: The Diary of Charlotte Forten, 1854.* Blue Earth Books, 2000.
Life in the North seen through the eyes of a free black girl in her teens

Biographies of Extraordinary Women

A biography recounts the life of a person who did something significant in the world. The biographies listed on the next page recount the lives of women who spent much of their adult lives committed to changing the world by fighting for equality of rights and opportunities for women, African Americans, Native Americans, the poor, and the oppressed. Others helped advance human knowledge in science and medicine. There are many other biographies written about extraordinary American women of the past and present.

Assignment

1. Read one of the suggested biographies on the Selected Biographies of Extraordinary American Women page or another biography approved by your teacher.

2. Prepare the answers to the Discussion Starters (below) based on the biography you read. Use these Discussion Starters as ideas for sharing with your reading circle or class or as the basis for a one-page essay about the person you chose.

Discussion Starters

1. Why was the subject of the biography you read important?

2. How did the experiences of the person's childhood and teen years affect her adult life?

3. What events, people, or ideas encouraged the subject of your biography to reform society or to become a leader in science, education, politics, medicine, or some other important work?

4. What leadership qualities did this woman demonstrate?

5. Describe how your subject displayed courage, loyalty, honesty, and faith.

6. What did your person accomplish in her life? Was she successful in her goals or did she fail?

7. What was the greatest challenge your subject faced?

8. Would you have liked to have known this woman? Explain your response.

1750   1800   1850   1900   1950   2000

Selected Biographies
of Extraordinary American Women

Most of these books will be available in public libraries along with many other excellent biographies of famous women.

Brown, Marion Marsh. *Susette La Flesche: Advocate for Native American Rights.* Children's Press, 1992.
Comprehensive and well-written story of the woman who led the fight for Indian citizenship

Brown, Sterling. *First Lady of the Air: The Harriet Quimby Story.* Tudor, 1997.
Good sketch of the life of this aviator

Collier, James Lincoln. *The Susan B. Anthony You Never Knew.* Children's Press, 2004.
Superior biography by a gifted children's writer

Fritz, Jean. *You Want Women to Vote, Lizzie Stanton?* Putnam, 1995.
Enjoyable biography of Elizabeth Cady Stanton

Gelletly, LeeAnne. *Harriet Beecher Stowe: Author of Uncle Tom's Cabin.* Chelsea, 2001.
Good account of the author's life and work

Harper, Judith E. *Maya Angelou.* The Child's World, 1999.
Clear outline of the poet's life

Herda, D.J. *Sandra Day O'Connor: Independent Thinker.* Enslow, 1995.
Excellent story of the justice's life and work

Jakoubek, Robert E. *Harriet Beecher Stowe.* Chelsea House, 1989.
Complete description of the abolitionist's career

Jezer, Marty. *Rachel Carson.* Chelsea House, 1988.
Detailed description of her life and work

Krull, Kathleen. *A Woman for President: The Story of Victoria Woodhull.* Walker, 2004.
An easy-to-read illustrated overview of Victoria's life

McPherson, Stephanie. *Sisters Against Slavery: A Story of Sarah and Angelina Grimke.* Carolrhoda, 1999.
Good review of the sisters' long careers

Meadows, James. *Marian Anderson.* The Child's World, 2002.
Clear, brief recital of the singer's life

Peck, Ira. *Elizabeth Blackwell: The First Woman Doctor.* Millbrook, 2000.
Brief, clear overview of Blackwell's career

Rubel, David. *Fannie Lou Hamer: From Sharecropping to Politics.* Silver Burdett, 1990.
Good, easy-to-read review of the life of this civil rights activist

Write Your Autobiography

Directions

1. Use the following outline as a cluster to help you create a short autobiography of your life.
2. Be as detailed about yourself as possible.
3. Be sure to describe your personal and career goals for the future.
4. Write your final draft in paragraph form.

Let Me Introduce You to . . .

Past to Present—First Paragraph

Birth (*time, place, circumstances*)

Life before school

Family (*people and pets*)

Grade school experiences (*special teachers, joyful events, successes*)

Favorite subjects

Special friends (*who they are and what you do together*)

Sports and hobbies

Present to Future—Second Paragraph

Personal strengths (*abilities and character*)

Career goals (*what you want to do with your life*)

Educational goals (*college and beyond*)

Personal goals (*family and life choices*)

Extension: Write Your Epitaph

- What would you like people to know about you when you have finished your life?
- What special thing would you like to be remembered for doing—as a public servant or member of the community?
- What epitaph would you want written on your tombstone?

Readers' Theater Notes

Readers' Theater is drama that does not require costumes, props, a stage, or memorization. It is done in the classroom by groups of students who become the cast of the dramatic reading.

Staging

Place an appropriate number of stools or chairs in a semicircle at the front of your class or in a separate staging area. Generally no costumes are used in this type of dramatization, but students dressed in similar clothing or colors can have a nice effect. Simple props can be used but are not required.

Scripting

Each member of your group should have a clearly marked script. Performers should practice several times before presenting the play to the class.

Performing

Performers should enter the classroom quietly and seriously. They should sit silently without moving and wait with their heads lowered. The first reader should begin, and the other readers should focus on whoever is reading, except when they are performing.

Assignment

Read the Readers' Theater: Bloomer Girls script chosen by your teacher about the suffragettes. Work with your assigned group to prepare for your performance, and share your interpretation of the script with your class.

Extensions

Write your own Readers' Theater script based on one of these events or another topic related to your study of extraordinary American women. Practice your script with a group of classmates, and then perform it for the rest of the class.

- Dorothea Dix tries to convince New York legislators to fund a school for girls.
- Belva Lockwood argues with judges for the right to practice before the Supreme Court.
- Susan B. Anthony debates with opponents about the rights of women to vote and control their own property.
- Victoria Woodhull argues with detractors over the idea of a woman president of the United States.
- Clara Barton talks to generals about the need for sanitation in army camps and hospitals.
- Sarah J. Hale tries to convince public leaders to support a national day of Thanksgiving or colleges for women.

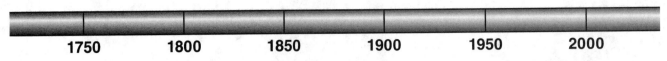

Readers' Theater: Bloomer Girls

This script records the reactions of people in the early 1850s to the women's rights movement and to a new style of clothing called "bloomers" championed by activists such as Susan B. Anthony and Elizabeth Cady Stanton. There are 12 speakers.

Narrator	Minister
Traditional Woman (Gladys)	Banker
Second Woman	Reporter
Elizabeth Cady Stanton	Judge Stanton
Amelia Bloomer	Farmer Jed
Susan B. Anthony	Farmer Elmer

Narrator: In the early 1850s a group of dedicated women are holding a rally in a New York community to encourage men and women to support several causes important to the new women's rights movement. These proposed rights would allow women to own and control their own property, to keep their own wages if they are employed, to travel freely, and most importantly, to vote. This meeting is marked by a daring new style of clothing, bloomers, which have been adopted by Amelia Bloomer, Elizabeth Cady Stanton, Susan B. Anthony, and some of their followers. Bloomers are a loose-fitting, comfortable style of women's pants. The crowd they have drawn is divided between one group of attentive women and a larger group composed of rowdy men and some traditionally dressed women who think the style looks like underwear.

Traditional Woman: Did you ever see such outrageous clothing? Bloomers, they call them. I call them indecent. What woman wants to go around wearing pants? I'd like to know!

Second Woman: It's absolutely shameful! These women are making a public spectacle of themselves. I wouldn't wear such a getup in the privacy of my own home, I'll tell you. My husband wouldn't allow it either, I'm happy to say.

Minister: It's scandalous! These women are parading around in unmentionables. It's absolutely deplorable! Deplorable, I say!

Readers' Theater: Bloomer Girls *(cont.)*

Banker:	The world's going crazy, I'll tell you that, Reverend. These women have no respect for themselves—it looks to me like they are dressed in their bedclothes! And you haven't heard the worst of it! You ought to hear some of the insane ideas these crazy ladies have hatched up. It's enough to make a decent man's head whirl.
Farmer Jed:	Elmer, I'm thinking of putting some of them there bloomers on my best milk cow, Bessie. She loves to be admired. Be better than on these here women.
Minister:	Mrs. Stanton, what possible excuse do you have for going about attired in such an indecent costume? Have you lost your mind?
Elizabeth Cady Stanton:	Well, sir, you have never had to wear 10 pounds of clothing while you did the cleaning, milked the cows, cooked dinner for a household, and cared for the baby. This costume, as you call it, will allow women to work more efficiently and with less fatigue. Petticoats and steel hoops are a curse!
Amelia Bloomer:	Look at those poor women over there. How do you think it is possible to carry a child and a candle upstairs at the same time while holding your hoopskirts to keep from tripping? I'd like to see any man manage that!
Traditional Woman:	I would like to lace my husband in with these blasted stays and wrap a steel hoop around him and see how well he milks a cow. Harold might have a different attitude if he had to wear a few pounds of petticoats, you can bet on that.

Readers' Theater: Bloomer Girls (cont.)

Second Woman: Oh, Gladys, that's awful!

But can't you just see my William trying to plow a field in a hoop?

Hee . . . hee . . . hee . . . What a perfectly terrible thought . . . I should be ashamed . . . but it might make him appreciate me more.

Reporter: Mrs. Stanton, you have been accused of preaching a revolution for women. What possible complaints could you ladies have? You are protected, provided for, and valued.

Elizabeth Cady Stanton: Slaves are protected and valued too—but they aren't free. A woman's place in society marks the level of its civilization. Just consider property rights. A woman who inherits property must turn it over to her husband. Women aren't legally allowed to manage their own estates. Even the wages earned by a seamstress or a maid belong to her husband.

Farmer Elmer: You just heard the terrible word—freedom. Next thing you know, women are going to want the freedom to do whatever they want. It's all downhill from there.

Susan B. Anthony: And a single woman's property is controlled by her father or brothers—even brothers who are little older than children!

Reporter: But everyone knows that females don't have the mental capacity to handle figures. It's a man's skill.

Second Woman: (aside to her friend) That is so ridiculous. My husband couldn't even read or do sums when we were married. I taught him.

Readers' Theater: Bloomer Girls *(cont.)*

Elizabeth Cady Stanton: Even a woman's household possessions and her clothes can be sold to pay off her husband's debt. Think of all the men going bankrupt or in debt every year. We couldn't possibly do any worse. And we'd be a lot less likely to drink or gamble away what we had.

Judge Stanton: That's my daughter Elizabeth. She certainly speaks well. What a pity she wasn't born a boy!

Farmer Jed: Did you get that, Elmer? Next thing you know, women will be putting us on an allowance and inquiring as to how much we lost in a card game or spent in the saloon. If they get control of the purse strings, it's gonna be the end of life as we know it.

Reporter: Mrs. Stanton, is it true that you want women to degrade themselves by trying to take jobs which only men can do—even in professions such as law and medicine and teaching?

Farmer Jed: Elmer, this is serious. Can you imagine women lawyers? Next thing you know, they'll want to be judges and congressmen. They'll be putting lace doilies on the spittoons and outlawing booze and swearing. Nobody can properly discuss public business without a few drinks under his belt and a little cussing.

Elizabeth Cady Stanton: Of course, there should be women doctors and lawyers and teachers— and news reporters too.

Reporter: News reporters! They want our jobs! That's absurd. No woman has the combination of stamina and intelligence to run down a story and evaluate the issues. The female brain isn't equipped to understand taxes or war.

Readers' Theater: Bloomer Girls (cont.)

Farmer Jed: With women reporters, all you'll ever get to read about are hairdos, dress styles, and unreasonable complaints about their husbands.

Farmer Elmer: You're right, Jed. It all started with reading. Women should never have been taught to read. It started them thinking, and that's always dangerous.

Reporter: Isn't it true that you radical women even want to vote? What woman has a mind capable of dealing with the complex issues of politics? What would the world come to?

Susan B. Anthony: The most ignorant male voter feels superior to any woman. Does one man have fewer rights than another because his intellect is inferior? Of course not.

So why should a woman be denied the right to vote? After all, how much worse could we make society? Look what men have already done with their wars, depressions, slavery, and drunkenness.

Banker: Equal rights will demoralize and degrade women who won't be able to handle them. It will prove a monstrous injury to all mankind.

Minister: This is just a petticoat revolution arranged by love-starved females. It's the most shocking and unnatural event in human history!

Elizabeth Cady Stanton: Most of our colleagues here are married, and many of our husbands support our cause. I have seven children of my own, and I keep as fine a home as any woman, I'll have you know.

Amelia Bloomer: Being married should not mean being tied to ignorance or strapped into a hoopskirt!

Readers' Theater: Bloomer Girls *(cont.)*

Susan B. Anthony: I know firsthand the problems of being a single woman. We unmarried women are scorned and pitied. I cannot even get served alone in most restaurants. Most hotels will not rent me a room—simply because I do not come attached to some male. Waiters will not even take a woman's order in a restaurant unless a man orders the meal—as if he knew what was best for her to eat.

Banker: But young lady, you need someone to protect you in this dangerous world. Surely some man will take pity on you and marry you if you drop this radical nonsense and get dressed!

Farmer Elmer: (aside) She's not that ugly—but too skinny for my taste.

Susan B. Anthony: A woman must not depend on the protection of men but be taught to protect and provide for herself. And I have had many offers of marriage, thank you!

I do not intend to be any man's property—nor do I intend to obey any man. The disgraceful laws of this state even allow a man to whip his wife as a punishment for disobedience.

Minister: Well, women and children do need to be corrected at times, of course. Otherwise, they wouldn't obey.

Farmer Elmer: If women didn't have to obey, they could do whatever they wanted!

Farmer Jed: What a terrible thought! Who would sew my buttons or cook dinner or darn my socks? I could die of starvation or frostbite!

Readers' Theater: Bloomer Girls (cont.)

Elizabeth Cady Stanton: Men tell us that we must be submissive and patient; that we must be womanly. What is a man's ideal of womanliness? It is to be quiet and obedient. These are beautiful virtues for children and feeble-minded adults. Weak and frivolous women have been created by customs and conventions. Men drill the spontaneity and imagination out of women.

We need to emancipate and liberate women to full equality with men. We need equal rights before the law and the right to vote!

Judge Stanton: Ah, if she'd only been a man.

Amelia Bloomer: Come on, ladies, let's raise our voices for equal rights for all men and women in America!

Farmer Jed: See, Elmer, I told you once women start to think, we're all headed for perdition. It'll be the end of civilization as we know it.

Narrator: By 1860, Susan B. Anthony and others had convinced the New York legislature to make some improvements in property rights for women, and gradual progress was made elsewhere as well. The right to vote was finally achieved by the ratification of the 19th Amendment to the Constitution in 1920.

| 1750 | 1800 | 1850 | 1900 | 1950 | 2000 |

Teacher Lesson Plans for Social Studies

Using Time Lines

Objective: Students will learn to derive information from a time line and make time lines relevant to them.

Materials: copies of Time Line of Extraordinary Women (page 73); reference materials including books, encyclopedias, texts, atlases, almanacs, and Internet sites

Procedure:

1. Collect available resources so that students have plenty of materials in which to find information.
2. Review the concept of a time line using the school year as an example.
3. Reproduce and distribute the Time Line of Extraordinary Women. Review the various events listed on the time line.
4. Instruct students to place additional dates on the time line as described in the assignment on page 73.
5. Students may want to use the readings from the beginning of the book to locate the 10 extra dates for their time lines.

Assessment: Verify the accuracy of the dates and events that students added to the time line. Assess students' ability to research other events to add to it.

Using Maps

Objective: Students will learn to use and derive information from maps.

Materials: copies of the Where They Came From map and list of extraordinary women (pages 74–76); atlases, almanacs, and other maps for reference; construction paper; scissors and glue

Procedure:

1. Reproduce and distribute the Where They Came From map pages. Review the information about famous women and the states they are associated with on page 76.
2. Review the map of the United States on pages 74–75. Ask students to identify a few states.
3. Have students cut out the sections of the map of the United States and assemble them on construction paper.
4. Label the map and use abbreviations to label the 50 states.
5. Add the number for each extraordinary woman (page 76) to the state where she was born, grew up, or lived as an adult.

Assessment: Correct the map activity together. Check for understanding and review basic concepts as needed.

Teacher Lesson Plans for Social Studies *(cont.)*

Understanding Suffrage

Objective: Students will recognize the significance of women's suffrage and the importance of exercising their own right to vote when they become adults.

Materials: copies of The Road to Suffrage (page 77) and Make Your Vote Count (page 78); books, encyclopedias, and Internet sources

Procedure:

1. Reproduce and distribute The Road to Suffrage. Review the women's suffrage time line and information. Assign the reflection essay and review the topics which are suggested.

2. Reproduce and distribute Make Your Vote Count. Review the information. Have students complete the activity.

3. Encourage students to reflect on the reasons some people don't vote and the reasons they should become voters when they reach adulthood.

Assessment: Encourage students to share their essays and responses.

Researching Famous American Women

Objective: Students will develop skills in finding, organizing, and presenting research information.

Materials: copies of Who Am I?—Hidden Heroines (page 79), Become an Extraordinary American Woman—or Influence (pages 80–82), and Extraordinary American Women (page 83); books, encyclopedias, and Internet sources

Procedure:

1. Have students use the Internet and books about American women to identify the women described on the Who Am I?—Hidden Heroines activity.

2. Review the information on Become an Extraordinary American Woman—or Influence. Discuss the outline on page 82 and the need to take notes to help prepare for the presentation. Review the guidelines carefully with your class. Indicate the many sources of information that you have collected.

3. Allow students to select a person from the list of Extraordinary American Women on page 83. Boys can present the famous woman from the viewpoint of a relative, friend, or opponent of the woman that they choose. Remind students that they need to find a significant amount of information about their heroines and then present the most important facts.

4. Give students time to research their person and prepare their famous person presentations. Arrange a schedule so that students can share with the class.

Assessment: Assess students on their oral classroom presentations as famous people, using the following categories and grading percentages or create a rubric of your choosing.

General Knowledge (50%) _____

Dramatic Skill (10%) _____

Voice (Loud/Clear) 20% _____

Costume (10%) _____

Notes (10%) _____

Time Line of Extraordinary Women

1773—Phillis Wheatley publishes her first book of poetry.

1776—Abigail Adams tells her husband to "remember the ladies."

1777—Sybil Ludington rides to warn Connecticut colonists that British troops are coming.

1782—Deborah Sampson joins Washington's army.

1814—Dolley Madison saves White House treasures from British.

1821—Emma Willard opens Troy Female Seminary.

1835—The Grimke sisters join the abolitionist movement.

1843—Sojourner Truth begins her career as a public speaker.

1846—Maria Mitchell discovers an unknown comet.

1849—Elizabeth Blackwell becomes the first modern woman doctor.

1849—Harriet Tubman escapes from slavery.

1852—*Uncle Tom's Cabin* by Harriet Beecher Stowe is published.

1853—Amelia Bloomer popularizes "bloomers."

1855—Lucy Stone becomes the first married woman to keep her maiden name.

1861—Sarah Edmonds joins the Union Army, becoming a soldier, spy, and nurse.

1864—Sarah J. Hale convinces President Lincoln to make Thanksgiving Day a national holiday.

1879—Mary Cassatt exhibits paintings with other Impressionists.

1879—Belva Lockwood becomes the first woman to practice before the Supreme Court.

1881—Clara Barton founds the American Red Cross.

1883—Sarah Winnemucca writes the first book by an American-Indian woman.

1889—Nelly Bly goes around the world in less than 80 days.

1889—Jane Addams founds Hull House to help poor city workers.

1902—Ida Tarbell investigates the Standard Oil Company.

1928—Margaret Mead publishes *Coming of Age in Samoa*.

1932—Amelia Earhart becomes the first woman to fly solo across the Atlantic Ocean.

—Eleanor Roosevelt begins her career as an activist first lady.

1939—Marian Anderson sings to 75,000 at the Lincoln Memorial.

1955—Rosa Parks sparks the Montgomery bus boycott.

1962—*Silent Spring* by Rachel Carson describes the dangers of chemicals used to kill insects and weeds.

1981—Sandra Day O'Connor becomes the first woman justice of the Supreme Court.

1983—Sally Ride becomes the first American woman in space.

1985—Wilma Mankiller becomes Chief of the Cherokee nation.

1986—Christa McAuliffe becomes the first teacher and private citizen to go into space (died in the Challenger explosion).

1993—Maya Angelou recites her poetry at the Clinton inauguration.

2009—Hillary Clinton becomes Secretary of State.

Assignment

Find at least 10 dates in United States history to add to this time line. These dates could include wars, assassinations, Presidential elections, inventions, disasters, cultural fads, sporting events, or other interesting historical occurrences. Then choose one of these events from the completed list to illustrate, color, and label on a separate sheet of paper. Be sure to include the date.

Where They Came From

Where They Came From *(cont.)*

Where They Came From (cont.)

Extraordinary American women came from many different states and some foreign nations. The list below indicates the states where these women were born, grew up, or lived as adults.

1. "Mother" Jones–TN
2. Alice Paul–NJ
3. Amelia Bloomer–NY
4. Amelia Earhart–KS
5. Anna Jarvis–WV
6. Anne Lindbergh–NJ
7. Anne Sullivan–MA
8. Annie Cannon–DE
9. Annie Oakley–OH
10. Barbara Jordan–TX
11. Barbara McClintock–CT
12. Belle Boyd–VA
13. Belle Starr–MO
14. Belva Lockwood–DC
15. Betty Ford—IL/MI
16. Betty Zane–WV
17. Billie Holiday–MD
18. Carrie C. Catt–WI
19. Carry Nation–KS
20. Christa McAuliffe–MA
21. Clara Barton–MA
22. Claudia Taylor Johnson–TX
23. Deborah Sampson–MA
24. Dian Fossey–CA
25. Dorothea Dix–ME
26. Elizabeth Blackwell–NY
27. Elizabeth Cady Stanton–NY
28. Emily Dickinson–MA
29. Emma Willard–NY
30. Fannie Lou Townsend Hamer–MS
31. Georgia O'Keeffe–NM
32. Geraldine Ferraro–NY
33. Grace Hopper–NY
34. Harriet Beecher Stowe–CT
35. Harriet Quimby–MI
36. Harriet Tubman–MD
37. Helen Keller–AL
38. Helen Thomas–KY
39. Hillary Clinton–NY/IL
40. Isadora Duncan–CA
41. Jane Addams–IL
42. Jeannette Rankin–MT
43. Juliette Low–GA
44. Katharine Graham–DC
45. Leontyne Price–MS
46. Lydia Darragh–PA
47. Madame C. J. Walker–LA
48. Mae Jemison–AL
49. Maria Mitchell–MA
50. Maria Tallchief–OK
51. Marian Anderson–PA
52. Mary Bethune–SC
53. Mary Bickerdyke–OH
54. Mary Cassatt -PA
55. Mary Chesnut–SC
56. Mary Jemison–NY
57. Nelly Bly–PA
58. Rachel Carson–PA
59. Rosa Parks–AL
60. Rose Greenbow–MD
61. Sacagawea–Idaho/ND
62. Sally Ride–CA
63. Sarah Caldwell–MO
64. Sarah Edmonds–MI
65. Sarah Grimke–SC
66. Sarah J. Hale–NH
67. Sarah Winnemucca–NV
68. Shirley Chisholm–NY
69. Susette La Flesche–NE
70. Susan B. Anthony–NY
71. Victoria Woodhull–OH
72. Wilma Mankiller–OK

Think About It—Which states seemed to have the most extraordinary women? Why do you think certain states had more representatives than others?

| 1750 | 1800 | 1850 | 1900 | 1950 | 2000 |

The Road to Suffrage

It took 80 years for women to win the right to vote. Originally, only some white men over 21 who owned property could vote. The right to vote gradually expanded, but it was 1920 before women could vote in national elections.

1848—First women's rights convention is held in Seneca Falls.

1851—Susan B. Anthony and Elizabeth Cady Stanton begin their long collaboration in the struggle for women's suffrage.

1869—Wyoming Territory grants women the right to vote.

—Lucy Stone creates American Women's Suffrage Association.

1872—Victoria Woodhull runs for President of the United States.

—Susan B. Anthony is arrested for voting in New York.

1884—Belva Lockwood runs for President of the United States.

1890—National American Woman Suffrage Association is formed.

1914—Montana grants suffrage to women.

1916—Carrie Chapman Catt leads final drive for women's suffrage with successful "Winning Plan" targeting both federal and state laws.

—Jeannette Rankin is the first woman elected to Congress.

1917—New York passes a referendum allowing women to vote.

1920—The 19th Amendment grants the right to vote to women.

—The League of Women Voters is formed.

The 19th Amendment

On August 18, 1920, Harry Burn, a young Tennessee representative, changed his vote in the Tennessee legislature. The legislature had deadlocked over the ratification of the 19th Amendment to the Constitution extending the right to vote to women. The young man was fulfilling a promise that he had made to his suffragette mother. His vote made Tennessee the 38th state to ratify the amendment, which thus became the law of the land.

Assignment—Reflecting on Women's Suffrage

Write an essay reflecting on the importance of women's suffrage on American society. Use evidence and your experiences to support your opinions. Mention how members of your family have been affected by the right to vote. Your essay should consider the following topics:

- Respect for the opinions and attitudes of women
- The effect of equal pay for women
- Childcare and issues related to raising children
- Military service for women
- Equal educational opportunities in high school and college
- Concern for the poor and underprivileged
- Equal job opportunities for women
- Discrimination in hiring and promoting women
- Positive and negative effects on men
- Opportunities in sports in school and college
- Election opportunities for women in government service such as U.S. senator, congresswoman, and president

1750   1800   1850   1900   1950   2000

Make Your Vote Count

Register to Vote

With a population of more than 300 million Americans, approximately 215 million are old enough to vote. This is about 70% of the population. About 140 million are registered to vote and therefore have a right to vote in local, state, and federal elections. Voters need to register when they turn 18 and when they move from one address to another. Voters can register by mail or in person at public offices like city clerk offices. Registration prevents voter fraud. A voter can only vote in one community and only once in an election.

Voter Requirements

The general requirements for voting are:

- You must be a citizen of the United States by birth or naturalization.
- You must be 18 or older.
- You must be registered to vote.
- You may not be convicted of a serious crime.

Why Don't People Vote?

- In the extremely close presidential election of 2000, only 54% of those old enough to vote cast a ballot. About 90 million people over the age of 18 didn't vote.

List three reasons why some people don't vote.

1. _____
2. _____
3. _____

Thinking About Your Right to Vote

List four issues that you think the local, state, or federal government needs to address to make your life better and your country a better place to live in. Tell what should be done about each issue.

1. _____
   _____
2. _____
   _____
3. _____
   _____
4. _____
   _____

Deciding to Vote

Give two reasons why you should register and vote when you turn 18 years old.

1. _____
   _____
2. _____
   _____

Who Am I?–Hidden Heroines

Mary Ann Bickerdyke	Margaret Corbin	Mother Ann Lee
Margaret Bourke-White	Sarah Edmonds	Sybil Ludington
Belle Boyd	Mary Jemison	Lucretia Mott
Elizabeth Cochrane	Mother Jones	Jeannette Rankin

Directions: Use the Internet and books about American women to match the women listed above with the statements below.

1. I was a soldier and spy for the Union Army during the Civil War.

   _____

2. I spent a lifetime battling for the rights of textile workers and coal miners.

   _____

3. I carried on a personal crusade with like-minded women against alcohol addiction in the early 1900s.

   _____

4. I traveled with American troops in Africa, Italy, and Germany as a war photographer during World War II.

   _____

5. I took over my husband's cannon after he was killed in a Revolutionary War battle in New York and was severely wounded during the fight.

   _____

6. I was a 16-year-old girl in 1777 who rode over 40 miles to warn the militia in the Connecticut countryside that British troops were preparing to attack.

   _____

7. I was a Quaker minister, abolitionist, and an agent of the underground railroad, helping fugitive slaves escape from their pursuers.

   _____

8. I was a courier (messenger) for Confederate generals and a spy who eavesdropped on the conversations of Union officers.

   _____

9. I was the founder of a new religious sect, the Shakers, and sometimes imprisoned for preaching in the streets.

   _____

10. As a child, I was captured by Shawnee Indians and became a respected leader among the Seneca tribe as an adult.

    _____

11. Using the name Nellie Bly, I traveled into very dangerous lands, worked in unsafe factories, and was locked up in a mental institution in order to report the truth to American readers.

    _____

12. I collected wounded soldiers from the battlefield and treated their injuries in Sherman's and Grant's armies through most of the Civil War.

    _____

Become an Extraordinary American Woman—or Influence

To truly understand the motivation, ideas, and success of these extraordinary American women, immerse yourself in the story of one person and become that person in your class. Choose a suffragette, soldier, spy, astronaut, adventurer, author, poet, pilot, political leader, or another interesting woman. Become familiar not only with the person but the times in which she lived. Become familiar with the issues of her time and acquire a sense of the day-to-day lifestyle of your heroine. Boys may choose to be the father, brother, friend, husband, or opponent of an extraordinary woman and present the life of a famous woman from his point of view.

Do the Research

1. Choose a woman from the list on page 83 or one that you have heard about. (Discuss your choice with your teacher if she is not on the list.) Read enough about the individual to make sure that it is someone who really interests you.

2. Use the research outline on page 82 to find out everything you can about the person. Know the important dates, the personal life, the accomplishments, and the failures of your character.

Go to the Sources

1. Use encyclopedias, almanacs, biographies, the Internet, and other sources to acquire basic information.

2. Find and use at least two full-length children's or young adult biographies about your person. You can also use adult biographies to research material not available in children's books.

3. Use the Index and Table of Contents of an adult biography to target specific information you need to know more about.

Take Careful Notes

- Use your own words. Don't copy sentences.

- Get all of the facts.

- Write down the facts in an orderly way. (The outline on page 82 is a good sample to use.)

- Look for anecdotes and funny stories about your person.

- Study the notes.

- Get a friend to quiz you about your person so that you know what you need to study and are confident about what you know.

- When other students are being questioned, write down the questions you couldn't answer about your own character and look up the answers later.

Become an Extraordinary American Woman—or Influence *(cont.)*

Get into Costume

- Put together an appropriate costume. Check your closets at home for long dresses, shirts, pajamas that could be turned into bloomers, or old costumes which might work.

- Boys can find dress coats and pants from older men.

- Check with parents, grandparents, older siblings, and friends for articles of clothing that might help. Ask for help getting to thrift stores for the missing pieces.

- Don't wear tennis shoes. (They weren't invented yet.) Use or borrow leather shoes. If they're too big, stuff them with tissue before putting them on for your presentation.

- Try to use a prop that fits with your character. These might include a poster for suffragettes, books for authors, bandages for medical workers, or some symbol associated with the person.

Be Famous

- Girls might start with this opening line:

  "My name is _____ . What would you like to know about me?"

- Boys might start with this opening line:

  "I personally knew _____ , one of the most _____ women you will ever meet. What would you like to know about her?"

- You might also want to give a brief presentation listing a few important facts about your famous woman. This will give your classmates a place to begin with their questions. Have a story to tell if there is a momentary lull in the questioning.

Stay in Character

- Don't forget who you are.

- Girls, you are an extraordinary American woman. Be that person. Assume the walk, the character, and the attitude of your person.

- Boys, you are a friend, relative, or even an opponent of a famous woman. Express your attitude, whether of admiration or disapproval, but tell the class everything about the woman you chose.

Be Dramatic

- You are not another student in the class. Be very serious. Avoid any silly behaviors.

- Use a loud voice. Don't drop your voice at the end of sentences.

- Use gestures. Use your arms and prop to emphasize your points.

- Take charge of the classroom. Stride across the front.

- Be forceful, assertive, and self-assured.

- Have confidence in yourself.

Become an Extraordinary American Woman—or Influence *(cont.)*

Research Outline

Directions: Use this outline to help you find important information about your extraordinary American woman.

I. Youth

a. Birth place and date

b. Home life and experiences

   1. Siblings (brothers and sisters)

   2. Places lived (parts of the country; farm or town)

   3. Circumstances (rich or poor; important events to your character)

c. Schooling (When?; How much?)

d. Childhood heroes, heroines, and/or supporters

e. Interesting facts and stories about your person's youth

II. Life Experiences

a. Experiences

   1. Describe the changes your character wanted to bring about in America or the world

   2. What actions your character took to convince people to support her (Describe each action and the results.)

   3. Problems your character faced (Give details.)

b. Lifestyle and personal habits

   1. Personal attitude toward life (List examples.)

   2. Values and principles she believed in

   3. Was she a risk-taker or cautious? (Give examples.)

   4. Personal behavior (cruel, kind, honest, etc.)

   5. Leadership experiences (Did people follow her? Why?)

c. Reasons for fame

   1. Accomplishments (name and describe successes)

   2. Challenges, failures, and things she didn't complete

   3. Greatest challenges she faced (Describe and explain.)

III. End of Life

a. Death

   1. Date of death/age at time of death

   2. Cause of death (facts about the death)

   3. Other facts about her death

b. Fame

   1. Was she famous at the time of her death?

   2. Was she admired or forgotten by the time of her death?

IV. The Life and Times

a. Contemporaries

   1. Other famous people she met or who were alive

   2. Presidents and public leaders of the time

b. Inventions and discoveries

   1. Important inventions of the time period

   2. Discoveries in medicine, science, or exploration

c. Travel and transportation

   1. How people traveled (boats, horses, other means)

   2. How goods and products were moved

Extraordinary American Women

Reformers

Jane Addams–labored to help poor in city slums
Marian Anderson–a voice for freedom
Maya Angelou–poetic voice for her people
Susan B. Anthony–leader in women's suffrage movement
Clara Barton–a true angel of the battlefield and much more
Amelia Bloomer–newspaper owner and suffragette
Nellie Bly–pioneer newspaper reporter
Rachel Carson–advocate for the environment
Carrie Chapman Catt–leader in final drive for suffrage
Catherine Coffin–helped many slaves reach freedom
Dorothea Dix–helped create asylums for the mentally ill
Angelina and Sarah Grimke–early opponents of slavery
Sarah Josepha Hale–first female magazine editor
Fannie Lou Hamer–civil rights activist
Alice Hamilton–campaigned for safer working conditions
Mary Jemison–Native American leader
Helen Keller–advocate for the disabled
Susette La Flesche–Native American advocate for citizenship
Wilma Mankiller–Cherokee chief
Lucretia Mott–abolitionist; "agent" of the Underground Railroad
Carry Nation–fierce advocate for temperance
Sandra Day O'Connor–first female justice of the Supreme Court
Rosa Parks–sparked the Montgomery bus boycott
Jeannette Rankin–first woman member of Congress
Elizabeth Cady Stanton–leading writer in suffrage movement
Harriet Beecher Stowe–abolitionist author
Sojourner Truth–former slave; abolitionist; suffragette
Harriet Tubman–a Moses for her people, former slave, conductor of the Underground Railroad
Emma Willard–advocate of women's education
Sarah Winnemucca–first American-Indian female author

Doctors, Scientists, Astronauts, and Aviators

Elizabeth Blackwell–first woman doctor of modern times
Emily Blackwell–second woman doctor
Bessie Coleman–first African-American female aviator
Amelia Earhart–the first lady of flight
Grace Hopper–computer pioneer
Mae Jemison–very talented doctor-astronaut
Christa McAuliffe–first teacher-astronaut
Margaret Mead–cultural anthropologist
Maria Mitchell–astronomer
Sally Ride–first American woman in space
Harriet Quimby–first licensed female airplane pilot

Heroines

Belle Boyd–daring Confederate spy
Lydia Darragh–her ride was as important as Paul Revere's
Sarah Emma Edmonds–Union soldier and spy
Annie Oakley–legendary marksman
Deborah Sampson–soldier in the American Revolution
Betty Zane–heroine of Fort Henry

Teacher Lesson Plans for Science and Art

Making Model Planes

Objective: Students will recognize the importance of pioneer women aviators and learn some of the principles of flight.

Materials: copies of Focus on the Aviators–Making Model Planes (pages 85–87); 8½" x 11" paper; small paper clips; tape; ruler

Procedure:

1. Reproduce and distribute Focus on the Aviators–Making Model Planes. Do each page in order.

2. Review the information on each aviator. Demonstrate the step-by-step process for making each plane. Stress each fold and use accurate measurements.

3. Designate a place for flying the planes. Paper planes fly better indoors, but some will work outdoors. Remind students to fly planes with a flip of the wrist.

Assessment: Ask students to demonstrate their planes and evaluate which models worked best.

Art

Objective: Students will recognize the painting styles of Mary Cassatt and Georgia O'Keeffe, and create similar compositions.

Materials: copies of Being Mary Cassatt (page 88); copies of Being Georgia O'Keeffe (pages 89–90); examples of Mary Cassatt's work, examples of Georgia O'Keeffe's work; art or construction paper, tempera paint, colored pencils, pastels, or colored markers; various flower samples

Procedure:

1. Reproduce and distribute Being Mary Cassatt. Display examples of her work. Help students study her style. Encourage them to create their own version of a Cassatt painting using the art supplies available.

2. Reproduce and distribute the Being Georgia O'Keeffe pages and provide flower samples.

3. Demonstrate how to carefully pull apart a sample flower. Review the parts of a flower and the terms. Have students illustrate and label the parts of a flower.

4. Distribute art supplies. Help students study the O'Keeffe illustrations on the page and encourage them to create their own version of an O'Keeffe painting on separate sheets of paper.

Assessment: If appropriate, have students share their artistic efforts in a gallery.

Using the Senses

Objective: Students will recognize how senses other than sight can be employed.

Materials: copies of Using Your Senses (page 91); dark handkerchiefs or bandanas, blindfolds, scarves; objects to identify

Procedure:

1. Reproduce and distribute Using Your Senses. Review the instructions with students. Stress safety and keeping the eyes completely covered.

Assessment: Ask students to describe their experiences and feelings as they did the activity.

Focus on the Aviators
–Making Model Airplanes

The three women highlighted on these pages broke down barriers for all women in aviation.

Assignment: Follow the directions on these pages to make paper planes that Harriet Quimby, Bessie Coleman, and Amelia Earhart would have loved.

Harriet Quimby (1875–1912)

Harriet Quimby was a writer for newspapers and magazines when she became interested in aviation in 1910. She became the first American woman pilot to qualify for a pilot's license. Dressed in bright, fashionable clothes that accentuated her good looks, Harriet was a popular participant in several aviation meets. She became the first woman to pilot a plane across the English Channel. During an air show in Boston on July 1, 1912, she lost control of her plane. Harriet and her passenger were thrown out of her plane and killed.

The Quimby Quickflyer

1. Fold an 8½ by 11-inch piece of paper the long way down the middle of the paper. Open the sheet.
2. Fold each corner from the top of the paper along the center line to make a triangle.
3. Fold the tip of the triangle down 2 inches.
4. Fold the top down 2 more inches.
5. Fold the paper along the center fold line again.
6. Measure ½ inch in from the center fold line on both sides of the fold line and draw a line.
7. Fold along each of these lines so that the wings extend out from the fold lines.
8. Measure ½ inch from the edges of each wing and fold the rudders up.
9. Place a small paper clip on the nose of the plane.
10. Launch the plane with a flip of the wrist.

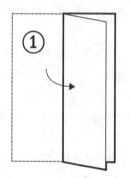
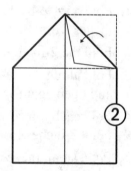
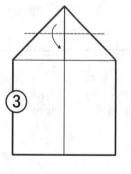
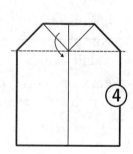
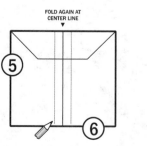
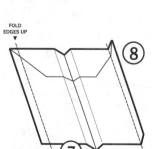
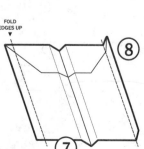
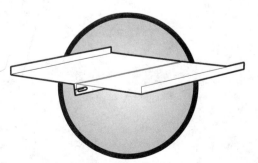

Focus on the Aviators
–Making Model Airplanes *(cont.)*

Amelia Earhart (1897–1937)

Amelia Earhart was born in Kansas, completed high school in Chicago, and worked as an army nurse in Canada during World War I. Despite her family's objections, she learned to fly in 1921 and soon bought her first plane. In 1928 she became the first woman to fly as a passenger across the Atlantic Ocean. In 1932 she became the first woman to fly solo across the Atlantic. In 1935 Amelia made the first solo flight from Honolulu to the U.S. mainland. Amelia wrote books and articles about her experiences. She became friends with First Lady Eleanor Roosevelt and gave her a plane ride. In 1937 Earhart attempted to complete an around-the-world flight with her copilot, Fred Noonan. On the last leg of the journey in the central Pacific, her plane developed trouble and radio contact was lost. No sign of her plane has ever been found.

Amelia's Airship

1. Fold an 8 ½ by 11-inch piece of paper down 2 inches from the top.

2. Fold the 2-inch piece down 2 more inches.

3. Fold along the center line to make a crease and open again.

4. Fold each top corner down to the center at the point 2 inches from the top.

5. Put a small piece of tape to hold the folds at the center.

6. Fold along the center line again and mark a line on each side 1½ inches from the center line.

7. Fold along these lines to make the fuselage and the wings.

8. Place one or two paper clips on the nose, and launch the plane with a flip of the wrist.

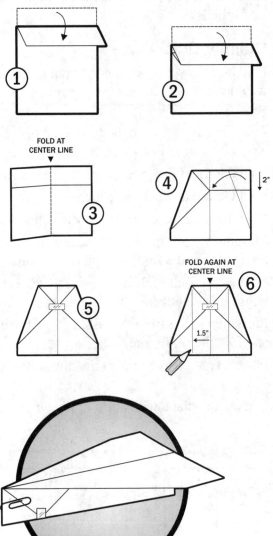

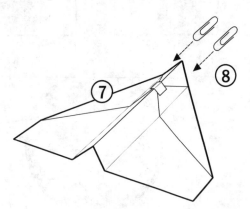

Focus on the Aviators
–Making Model Airplanes *(cont.)*

Bessie Coleman (1892–1926)

Bessie Coleman was the first African-American woman pilot. Born to extreme poverty in 1892 in Texas, Bessie attended school when she wasn't picking cotton. Bessie was determined to fly planes, and when no flight school in America would accept her, she went to France, learned to fly, and earned an international pilot's license. She came back to the United States and did barnstorming aerial shows in borrowed airplanes using her good looks and personality to attract spectators. Bessie impressed crowds with her skill as a pilot and her courage as a stunt person. She finally was able to purchase a plane, but it wasn't very airworthy, and she crashed breaking her leg and three ribs. Bessie was later killed during a practice flight in Florida.

Bessie's Barnstormer

1. Fold the top of an 8½ by 11-inch piece of paper down to 2 inches from the bottom.

2. Fold the paper in half down the middle.

3. Fold each corner over along the center line, making a triangle at the top of the plane.

4. Fold each side of the triangle in half again down the center line, making a very pointed triangle.

5. Place a small paper clip below the nose to keep the folds tight and provide weight.

6. Launch the plane with a flip of the wrist.

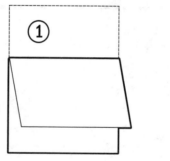

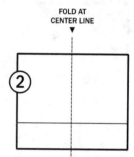

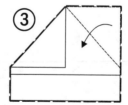

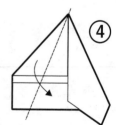

Design Your Own Plane

Use the skills you developed on these pages to make your own planes.

You may want to make variations of the planes on these pages by changing one or two folds or using different measurements for the folds.

Test fly each plane and notice which ones work best.

Have a good flight!

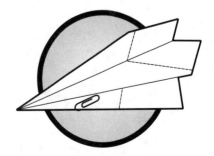

Being Mary Cassatt

Mary Cassatt used bright, vivid colors with many of her artistic compositions. She favored women and children as her subjects.

Directions:

1. Research Mary Cassatt's paintings. Observe her subject matter, choice of colors, and style.
2. Create your own Mary Cassatt composition. If you wish, choose a friend to act as a model.
3. Pencil in the sketch below.
4. Use colored pencils, pastels, or colored markers to provide the color.

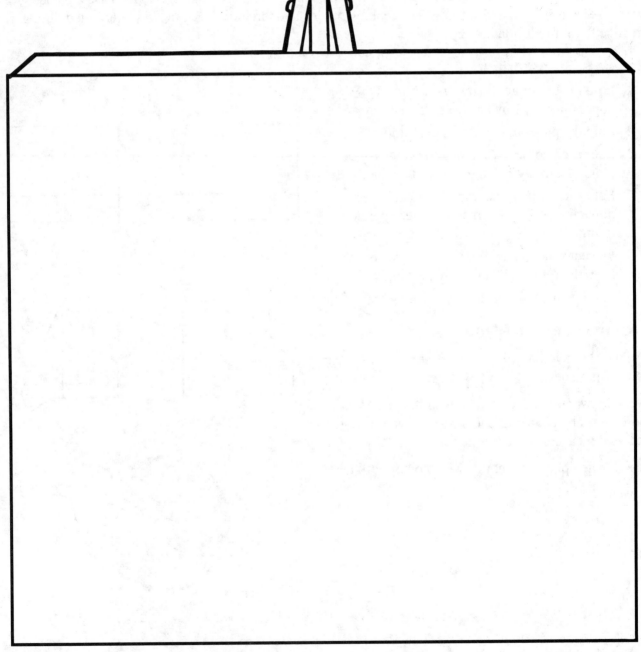

Being Georgia O'Keeffe

Georgia O'Keeffe was especially famous for her desert scenes and for the exceptionally detailed and vibrant flowers in her compositions.

Directions:

1. Review the parts of a flower illustrated on this page and the explanations for each term.
2. Collect several flowers from home.
3. On a separate sheet of paper, draw an illustration of one flower and label the parts that are visible.
4. Carefully dissect the flower and find as many parts as you can identify from the illustration. Not all flowers are alike. Some parts may be missing or modified on different types of flowers.

Parts of a Flower

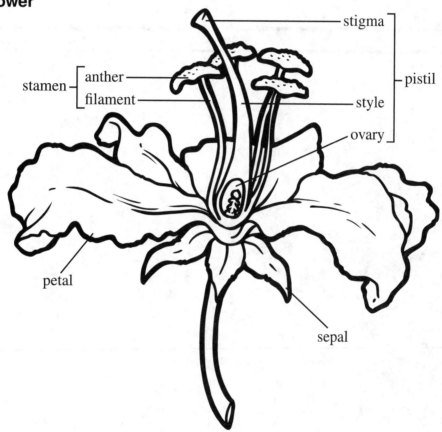

Terms

anther–part of the stamen which produces pollen

filament–thin stem that supports the anther

stamen–the male part of a flower made up of the anther and filament

petal–brightly colored outer part of a flower

sepal–small green leaf which protects the bud

style–tube-shaped part that holds up the stigma

ovary–place where seeds develop

stigma–sticky part at the top of a flower where pollen grains catch and hold

pistil–the female part of the flower which includes the stigma, style, and ovary

Being Georgia O'Keeffe *(cont.)*

Georgia O'Keeffe was famous for her paintings of desert scenes and flowers.

Directions

1. Research Georgia O'Keeffe's paintings.
2. Create your own Georgia O'Keeffe composition. Arrange flowers or a desert scene of your own.
3. Pencil in the sketch below.
4. Use colored pencils, pastels, or colored markers to provide the color.

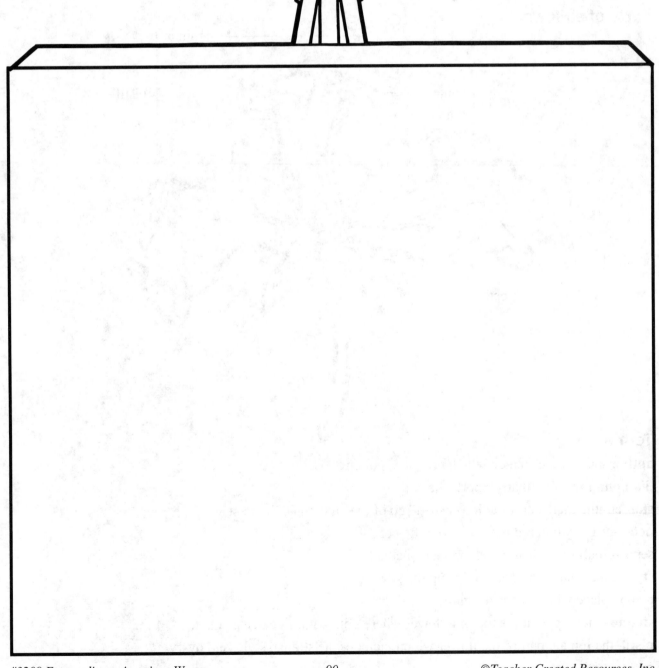

Using Your Senses

Helen Keller

Helen Keller was a healthy toddler who was infected with a fever when she was 19 months old. The infection left Helen blind, deaf, and mute. She was examined by Alexander Graham Bell when she was six. He sent a remarkable woman named Anne Sullivan to work with Helen. Anne became Helen's teacher and lifelong companion. Helen eventually attended Radcliffe College, learned to speak intelligibly, and became a lifelong advocate and role model for the blind and the disabled.

Becoming Sightless

Persons who are blind learn by using their other senses, and often, these other senses are heightened. Do this activity to appreciate their experiences.

Materials: dark handkerchiefs, or bandanas, blindfolds, or scarves; objects to identify

Directions:

1. Work with a partner.
2. One partner will place a dark handkerchief or bandana across the eyes of the other and tie it in place around his or her head.
3. The partner who can see should lead the "blind" partner to the stations listed below. Note: Instruct the "leaders" to be very careful when guiding partners. Make certain that where they are walking and what they might pick up or touch is safe.
4. The blindfolded partner should examine each object with his or her fingertips, listen for any sound it might make when touched, and smell each object. He or she should then try to guess the name of the object.
5. Have students switch roles after one partner has done the stations.

Station One—Student Desk

Have the sightless partner carefully remove the contents of the desk. The "blind" student should examine each object and guess its identity which the partner can write on the chart.

Actual Name of Object   **Guess**

_____   _____

_____   _____

_____   _____

_____   _____

Station Two—Around the Room and Outside the Room

The "blind" student should be escorted around the room and try to identify classroom materials, science materials, playground equipment, books, and similar objects in the same manner as above. Then go outside for further experiences.

Actual Name of Object   **Guess**

_____   _____

_____   _____

_____   _____

_____   _____

Celebrate Women's History Day

If possible, set aside one day to be devoted to activities related to your study of American women. You might call it Women's History Day. Try doing this activity with two or three classes at the same grade level. This allows you to share some of the responsibilities and provides a special experience for the entire grade level. (Note: These activities can be done independently of a special day.)

Costumes

Encourage each girl to dress in a costume that reflects the famous American woman that she chose for her research project. The boys should come as the relatives, friends, or famous men they researched when doing the project.

Parent Help

Encourage as many parents or older siblings as you can to come for all or part of the day to enjoy the proceedings and to help set up and monitor the activities. This is truly a day involving the family in the educational process. It helps to survey parents ahead of time to discover any special talents, interests, or hobbies that would be a match for specific centers.

Notes on Planning Centers

- The centers you set up should relate in some way to the history of American women.
- Centers should involve the children in doing an activity and often in making something they can take or put on display.
- The class should be divided into groups with about six or seven students per group.
- Each center should take about 20 minutes. Students can then rotate to the next activity.
- The following suggestions will get you started. You will want to add any others for which you have special expertise.

Doing Portraits

Each student should do a portrait of one extraordinary woman. You will need to have pictures available of many of these women for the students to copy. You might also have your girls in costume serve as models of these women while other classmates do their portraits. You will need 9 by 12 inch pieces of white drawing or construction paper, dark lead pencils, colored pencils, or colored markers.

Quiz Show

Have students write questions (with answers) to be asked to individual students or teams in a quiz show format like Jeopardy.

The questions could be done ahead of time and given to the master of ceremonies.

Dancing

A simple square dance or line dance can be learned or practiced in the 20 minutes allotted for each center. At least one volunteer parent or teenager would be needed as a teacher.

| 1750 | 1800 | 1850 | 1900 | 1950 | 2000 |

Celebrate Women's History Day *(cont.)*

Clay Figures or Busts

In this center, students can use modeling clay or rectangular blocks of inexpensive sculpting clay to make figures or busts of some of the heroines they studied. A 25-pound bag of sculpting clay can be sliced into 18 or more rectangular blocks of clay with a piece of fishing line. Use toothpicks to carve the features. Have paper towels available for clean up.

Readers' Theater

The Readers' Theater center involves practicing with a script for a Readers' Theater presentation. The script could be the one in this book or one that students have written for the occasion. Students at this center could collaboratively write and perform a script.

Getting Around

Transportation is an important part of life in any era. Students could use this center to recreate one method of transportation used during the lifetime of the famous woman they studied. Use small boxes, straws, craft sticks, modeling clay, and other materials to create cars, boats, wagons, stagecoaches, spaceships, airplanes or similar methods of transportation.

Learn a Game

Set up indoor and/or outdoor centers with some games from earlier eras. These might include chess and checkers; baseball (played by the earlier rules); tennis for modern women like Sally Ride; and card games like Old Maid, Whist, and Gin Rummy. Games of tag and hide-and-seek were popular throughout the last two centuries. Old-fashioned basketball played with a peach basket on a pole became popular at the turn of the 20th century.

Poetry Center

This center could have a large number of narrative poems in duplicate copies. Teams of students could prepare a poem in two voices that they haven't done before or present one they did during this project. Parents and other students would be the audience.

Read a Book

Students sometimes appreciate a quiet reading center as an activity break. Books by popular children's authors or short, easy, stories would allow children a quiet period between more active centers.

Build a Monument

Students can design and build a monument as a tribute to one famous American woman. The monument might be a statue, a building which represents her accomplishments, a home or school, or some other model. This center could have modeling clay, craft sticks, construction paper, and other craft items. Students may use pictures from this book or other sources for ideas or models.

Eat Healthy

If you have parent volunteers, plan a luncheon with a women's suffrage rally or a similar theme. Parents and students could do the decorations together at one of the centers.

Annotated Bibliography

Nonfiction

Armstrong, Jennifer. *The American Story: 100 True Tales from American History*. Knopf, 2006. (Interesting vignettes about men and women in American history.)

Bausum, Ann. *Our Country's First Ladies*. National Geographic, 2007. (Very fine overview of each first lady and her accomplishments.)

Briggs, Carole S. *Women in Space*. Lerner, 1999. (Good account of the accomplishments of female astronauts.)

Chang, Ina. *A Separate Battle: Women and the Civil War*. Scholastic, 1991. (Exceptional overview of the important roles women played in the war.)

Chin-Lee, Cynthia. *Amelia to Zora: Twenty-Six Women Who Changed the World*. Charlesbridge, 2005. (Exceptionally well-written and illustrated introduction to some of the dynamic women of the 20th century.)

Coleman, Penny. *Adventurous Women: Eight True Stories About Women Who Made a Difference*. Holt, 2006. (Excellent accounts of the work of Alice Hamilton, Mary McLeod Bethune, and Biddy Mason.)

Currie, Stephen. *Women Inventors*. Lucent, 2001. (Excellent review of the work of Grace Hopper, C.J. Walker, and others.)

Hansen, Joyce. *Women of Hope*. Scholastic, 1998. (Superb introduction to African-American women from the Delaney sisters to Mae Jemison.)

Harness, Cheryl. *Remember the Ladies: 100 Great American Women*. HarperCollins, 2001. (Very colorful introduction to 100 interesting American women from Virginia Dare to Ruth Simmons.)

Lowery, Linda. *One More Valley, One More Hill: The Story of Aunt Clara Brown*. Random House, 2002. (Superb story of one black woman's success as a business woman and long search for her daughter.)

Lunardini, Christine. *What Every American Should Know About Women's History: 200 Events that Shaped Our Destiny*. Bob Adams, 1994. (Excellent brief accounts of pivotal events in the history of American women.)

Vare, Ethlie Ann and Greg Ptacek. *Women Inventors & Their Discoveries*. Oliver, 1993. (Good accounts of inventive women who created new plants, computer languages, foods, and other specialized products.)

Webster's Dictionary of American Women. Smithmark, 1996. (The best, most accurate, and most complete biographical encyclopedia of American women in one volume.)

Welden, Amelie. *Girls Who Rocked the World*. Beyond Words, 1999. (Clever, brief vignettes of 32 interesting women of the world.)

Wilkinson, Brenda. *African American Women Writers*. Wiley, 2000. (Good account of poets and writers from Phillis Wheatley to Alice Walker.)

Poetry

Burns, Marjorie (ed.). *The Charge of the Light Brigade and Other Story Poems*. Scholastic, 1990. (Great compendium of ballads and story poems to use for poetry in two voices.)

Glossary

abolitionist–a person opposed to slavery

activist–a person determined to create change

allies–people on the same side of a conflict

amendment–a change to a law or framework of laws, such as the Constitution of the United States

anthropologist–a person who studies the culture and beliefs of different peoples

attorney general–the highest legal officer of a state or nation

autobiography–the story of a person's own life

aviatrix–a woman pilot

barnstorming tour–to put on air shows in many cities

bloomers–long baggy pants narrowing at the ankles worn below or instead of a skirt

boycott–when people, for political reasons, refuse to buy a product

candidate–a person running for public office

capital–the city where the government meets

convention–a meeting where people can promote a cause such as women's rights

emancipation–to free slaves

freedom marchers–people who demonstrated for African American civil rights

Great Depression–period of severe economic decline and unemployment in the United States from 1929 to 1940

headmistress–principal or person in charge of a school

infirmary–a place for the care of the sick; a small hospital

insane asylum–a place of confinement for the mentally ill

Jim Crow laws–state and local segregation laws enacted in the South after the Civil War; practice of segregating black people in the U.S.

legislature–group of lawmakers who make, change, and repeal laws

pacifist–a person opposed to war

patent–ownership rights to an invention

petticoats–long, heavy garments worn under a dress in the 18th and 19th centuries

Prohibition–a period from 1919 to 1933 when the sale of alcohol was illegal in the United States

Quakers–members of a religion opposed to war and slavery

reformer–an individual committed to changing society

secede–the decision of a state to leave the Union

segregation–separation based on race or sex

seminary–a private school for young women

slave–person who is owned by another person

sojourner–wanderer; traveler

spiritualism–the system of belief that one can communicate with the spirits of the dead

suffrage–the right to vote in elections

suffragettes–women who worked for the right of women to vote

temperance–opposition to alcohol use

zealous–strong support of a movement or belief

Answer Key

Page 34
1. c	6. d
2. c	7. c
3. d	8. c
4. a	9. a
5. b	10. d

Page 35
1. d	6. d
2. d	7. c
3. a	8. c
4. a	9. b
5. c	10. b

Page 36
1. c	6. d
2. d	7. b
3. c	8. c
4. b	9. d
5. c	10. b

Page 37
1. c	6. b
2. a	7. b
3. b	8. d
4. d	9. b
5. c	10. b

Page 38
1. b	6. c
2. c	7. c
3. c	8. b
4. b	9. a
5. a	10. d

Page 39
1. c	6. a
2. b	7. a
3. d	8. d
4. c	9. d
5. c	10. b

Page 40
1. b	6. c
2. d	7. d
3. a	8. b
4. c	9. a
5. d	10. a

Page 41
1. a	6. d
2. c	7. a
3. b	8. c
4. b	9. b
5. d	10. d

Page 50
1. suffragettes; suffrage
2. reformers (or activists)
3. Amendment
4. spiritualist; candidate
5. Quaker; abolition; emancipation
6. freedom marcher; voters' rights
7. seminary
8. temperance
9. insane asylums
10. Convention; legislatures

Page 52

Across
1. abolitionist
3. emancipation
7. equal
10. suffragettes
11. custody
12. patent
13. seminary

Down
1. amendment
2. tenements
4. protest
5. Quaker
6. sojourn
8. legislature
9. feminist

Page 55

1. List the rhyming words of each stanza.

1st stanza-	Lord	stored	sword
2nd stanza-	camps	damps	lamps
3rd stanza-	steel	deal	heel
4th stanza-	retreat	judgement-seat	feet
5th stanza-	sea	me	free

2. What pattern can you find?

The words ending the second, fourth, and sixth lines in each stanza rhyme.

3. Does every end word in a stanza have a rhyming partner?

No—only the end of the second, fourth, and sixth lines rhyme.

Page 56

1. **Verse:** "They have builded him an alter in the evening dews and damps…" *is compared* to the night camps and watch fires of the soldiers as if they were preparing an alter for God as they get ready to fight.

2. **Verse:** "He is trampling out the vintage where the grapes of wrath are stored…" *is compared to* the act of God making wine by crushing the grapes (of righteous anger) with his feet as He and the soldiers will crush the enemy.

Find this simile.

"As we deal with my contemners, so with you My grace shall deal…" *is comparing* the actions of the soldiers with the enemy with the power and grace of God in dealing with the soldiers.

"America the Beautiful"

Write the rhyming words from each stanza.

1st stanza	skies	majesties	(visual)
	grain	plain	(sound)
2nd stanza (Chorus)	thee	sea	(sound)
3rd stanza	feet	beat	(sound)
	stress	wilderness	(sound)
4th stanza (Chorus)	flaw	law	(sound)
5th stanza	proved	loved	(visual)
	strife	life	(sound)
6th stanza (Chorus)	refine	divine	(sound)
7th stanza	dream	gleam	(sound)
	years	tears	(sound)
8th stanza (Chorus)	thee	sea	(sound)

Note: Rhyme may be either oral (sound) such as dream and gleam or visual (sight) such as skies and majesties.

Page 79
1. Sarah Edmonds
2. Mother Jones
3. Jeannette Rankin
4. Margaret Bourke-White
5. Margaret Corbin
6. Sybil Ludington
7. Lucretia Mott
8. Belle Boyd
9. Mother Ann Lee
10. Mary Jemison
11. Elizabeth Cochrane
12. Mary Ann Bickerdyke